OLD TIMES IN THE
FAULKNER COUNTRY

OLD TIMES IN THE FAULKNER COUNTRY

BY

JOHN B. CULLEN

IN COLLABORATION WITH

FLOYD C. WATKINS

LOUISIANA STATE UNIVERSITY PRESS
Baton Rouge

ISBN 0-8071-0099-4
Library of Congress Catalog Card No. 61-1874
Copyright© 1961 by the University of North Carolina Press
All rights reserved
Manufactured in the United States of America
Reissued January 1975 by Louisiana State University Press
by special arrangement with the
University of North Carolina Press

1976 Printing

Contents

Introduction

"THE ARTIST," William Faulkner has said, "is influenced by all in his environment. He's maybe more sensitive to it because he has to get the materials, the lumber that he's going to build his edifice with." In this statement Faulkner has described two worlds: one is the edifice, the fiction, the world that he has made, the product of his creative imagination. The other is Faulkner's environment, "his own experience of people," what he has called "the lumber in the attic."

Perhaps to the pure critic "the lumber" is unimportant, because the final edifice is not the original forest. But the relationship between the two worlds has been a major subject of dispute among Faulkner's readers. One group goes so far as to deny that Faulkner is writing about the South. Instead, they say, he is creating a world of universal values, a myth of modern times; his books are primarily philosophical and psychological and aesthetic creations, and only accidentally considerations of the problems of the South. The sociologist and the historian see in the books a treatment of Southern life or of cultural patterns of the Western world. But the Southerner sees his South, and if he is from Mississippi, especially from Lafayette County, he may see only his own community in Faulkner's works.

In a time of expatriate American writers and displaced or fugitive Southerners, the world of William Faulkner is extraordinarily identifiable. Faulkner grew up in Oxford, a small town and the county seat of Lafayette County in the northern hilly regions of Missisippi. In Oxford he has remained except for brief trips, some youthful wanderings, and occasional sojourns in such places as New Orleans, Hollywood, and Virginia. His environment, the source of the lumber in the attic, is Mississippi, Lafayette County, and Oxford—the history, mores, folklore, traditions, and attitudes of a rather small, apparently stereotyped, yet almost infinitely varied rural community. The world in a grain of sand.

In the summer of 1957 I visited Oxford for the first time, hoping to find the lumber in the attic, to meet Faulkner's friends and neighbors, to discover what he had found to write about in this provincial town. Jefferson is Oxford, the local gossips who have read Faulkner's works will say, but Jefferson is Oxford transmuted; the lumber is not the edifice. And the process of change from the real Lafayette County to Faulkner's Yoknapatawpha County is complex. The trees that make the lumber have been cut down and sawed and planed and nailed and painted. The construction of fiction is more Faulkner's than it is the town's, but the lumber is still there. Tracing all the books back to Faulkner's environment would prove as difficult as putting the boards back in the trees. No single citizen knows all that Faulkner knows about life in the county, and none of his friends has read all of his books. An outsider, a scholar probing the attics of the county's past, can hardly hope to acquire a knowledge of its actual history and geography which equals his knowledge of Faulkner's works.

Reading old files of local newspapers, I noticed a copy of a letter from one of Faulkner's hunting companions to the King of Sweden, who had awarded Faulkner the Nobel Prize. Faulkner's friend, John Cullen, invited His Majesty to join the hunt in the Mississippi River bottoms and to feast on such backwoods delicacies as coon and collards. Here, I thought, was a man who might tell me some of the things I wished to know about Faulkner and his environment.

So I asked the way to John Cullen's, drove out a dozen miles or so on the highway to New Albany, turned off onto a dirt country road, then onto a still smaller road, and finally onto a small driveway which ran through large trees back to an unpainted farmhouse. John Cullen lay asleep under a large oak tree in the yard. Deep-voiced hounds barked at me, and my host waked from his bed of boards which lay across two sawhorses.

During that afternoon Cullen showed me his experiments with grafting fruit trees, gave me a peck of tomatoes from his "truck crop," took me down to a spring for a cold drink of water, introduced me to his dogs, told hundreds of jokes and stories, and answered dozens of questions about Faulkner and about Lafayette and Yoknapatawpha counties. When I left just before dark, I carried with me the peck of tomatoes and copies of the hundreds of folksy columns Cullen has written for the Oxford *Eagle*.

This was the first of several afternoons with John Cullen. He lives alone with his dogs and plants surrounded by a vast area of government forests. His wife is dead, and his son is in the army.   Except for a pickup truck, trips to town, and visitors who bring the modern world to his farm, his life is as simple and rustic as the ways of the Bundrens and McCallums in Faulkner's novels.   But that is the way he wants it.

I went to John Cullen's to get materials to write a book on William Faulkner.   But my book became John's, because he knows Faulkner's lumber in the attic.   Since the summer of 1957 John has been writing me letters.   Often he has risen early, even for the country, on a cold winter morning, built a wood fire, and written by lamplight with the inspiration of a jug of corn whisky.   After the writing and a properly stimulating amount of the liquor, he has cooked his breakfast.

John is a good talker and story-teller, a folk humorist, a yarn-spinner, in the tradition of Mark Twain. Good folk talkers are seldom good writers.   Pencil in hand, they freeze and lose their personality.   But John is different.   He can put his humor and wisdom on paper.   This book is compiled mainly from his letters, but I have supplemented these from extensive notes based on conversations with John and his friends, and from transcriptions of about eight recording sessions of two to four hours each in June, 1959.   "Big Red" Bright and Walton ("Uncle Bud") Miller joined in one of these sessions, and a few paragraphs derive ultimately from their conversation.   Here and there, I myself have written a short paragraph based on my own knowledge of Lafayette County and of the works of William Faulkner.   This collaboration does not affect the authenticity of the book any more than retelling affects the authenticity of an old folk tale. What I have done is to supply the order, sometimes the language, and occasionally the knowledge that make out of John's recollections a whole, consistent document. He knows the gaps are there; he has kindly allowed his Oxford friends and me to fill them when we could.

John has read several versions of the complete manuscript, has made suggestions for revision, and approves it entirely as it is here presented. I have taken every care that this book remain true to the standard of integrity established by John's Author's Note, which is drawn wholly from his letters.

John Cullen has now read much of Faulkner, but when I first met him he had read only a novel or so and several short stories. It is impossible to be precise about the exact extent of his knowledge of Faulkner's work because, like many another reader, he had started many more stories than he had finished and was later not certain of how far he had read. I know that some of the tales he tells were written after he read Faulkner's work. For instance, his story of his encounter with a girl like Temple Drake in the Memphis whorehouse was written after he had read *Sanctuary*. On the other hand, the story of the lynching of Nelse Patton (part of the lumber in the attic for the story of Joe Christmas in *Light in August*) was written before he had read the novel.

The complexity of John's views of William Faulkner results in inconsistency and seeming self-contradiction. There is Faulkner the man and Faulkner the writer, and to the people of Oxford the two are not the same. Even Faulkner the man is "hard to figure," they say. He is a gracious host one evening, and the next day he does not speak to them on the streets of the town. He is arrogant, and he is humble.

He is a good friend on a hunting trip, but so quiet and reserved that no one ever knows him. Faulkner the writer has in the outside world a reputation which is inconceivable in his own country. He has written stories his neighbors like, published novels they cannot understand, and created Southern characters they consider insulting. This is the paradox that explains some of John's views on his friend and neighbor.

One of Cullen's intentions is to retell the folk tales used by Faulkner in his fiction. This book is partly a telling of the background facts of the Yoknapatawpha legend, but Cullen's stories are also more than the facts. He himself has exaggerated and transmuted. Much of what Faulkner has known about life in his county has of course come from legend and folklore rather than from witnessing at first hand. Even many of Faulkner's techniques are ultimately derived from those of the folk yarn-spinner. The spirit of the practical joker, the tall tale, the lurid image and vivid figure of speech, the ridiculous situation, the brutality—these are the common basis of backwoods humor, the works of William Faulkner, and this book by John Cullen. And this is no discredit to Faulkner, for the very similarities seem to emphasize the extent of his accomplishments. Some of the characteristics of Cullen's style help to explain some of the intricacies of Faulkner's prose. Rural dialect in Cullen's writing resembles that in Faulkner's, but almost astonishing in this book is Cullen's occasional blending of dialect with polysyllabic words and rhetorical flourishes. Faulkner's own development of unsophisticated characters and their dialect in a context of sophisticated themes and polysyllabic diction may be a refinement of the practice of the folk tale-teller.

Cullen does not think of himself as a poor man's William Faulkner. Again, some of the weaknesses of this book demonstrate the remarkable accomplishments in the Yoknapatawpha cycle. But John Cullen's book is in itself unique. It is, so far as I know, the only biographical and literary study of a great living writer ever written by an intelligent and unschooled friend and neighbor.

In a larger sense, this is Oxford's book about Faulkner, and to many of the citizens there, John's friends and mine, the books owes a debt for information and comment which might otherwise have gone unrecorded. Another community, Emory University, has made many contributions, including generous support by the University Research Committee.

Floyd C. Watkins

Author's Note

WILLIAM FAULKNER and I have been friends since we were little boys. Both of us grew up in Oxford, Lafayette County, Mississippi, where we have lived most of our lives. We have heard the same stories and known the same people, and in his fiction Faulkner has often written about the things we have known. I do not understand many things in Faulkner's writing, and I doubt very much that anyone else does or ever will. But I do know him and the backgrounds of his fiction. In this book I plan to tell some of the stories as I have heard them told or seen them happen, and I hope to describe Faulkner in his native environment. In practically every story which I have read about Faulkner's fictitious Yoknapatawpha County, I have recognized many of the locations and the characters. Faulkner has retold the county's stories so well that I ought not to tell them again. But my versions are different from Faulkner's at times, and the inferiority of my tales may prove the greatness of his. I am not posing as one of Faulkner's closest friends and confidants. I think he would resent that.

Several things lately have inspired me to think that I can be a writer. Recently in an old *Look* magazine I saw some pictures of a Negro sculptor who was selling for fantastic prices his crude, childish carvings. But the thing that inspires me most is a monkey in the zoo in New York. When given brush and paint, he paints great works which sell for hundreds of dollars. Perhaps I can write something of interest to our great public.

John B. Cullen

OLD TIMES IN THE
FAULKNER COUNTRY

I

Young Faulkner and His Family

MY FIRST MEMORIES of William Faulkner date back to the times when I used to pass his home on my way to and from school. He lived on a wide shady street now known as South Lamar, but then called South Street. The Falkner[1] children had a spotted pony and almost every kind of toy and gun that children could have in those days. William and his brothers, John, Murry, and Dean, had no sister, but their cousin Sallie Murry Wilkins was reared by Faulkner's parents. Usually when I passed by, the Falkner boys and Sallie were playing on the street. At that time there was little danger in children using the streets as a playground. Few in Oxford had ever seen an automobile. The future Mrs. William Faulkner, Estelle Oldham, was one of William's childhood playmates. The Falkner and the Oldham children were friendly and pleasant even toward me, a country jake. Everyone liked them.

William Faulkner was a little fellow when I went to school, about two grades behind me and small for his age. On the school ground he stood around a great deal, and I never saw him play many games with

[1] The Falkner family still spell their name without a *u*, but William has restored the letter dropped by his great-grandfather.

other children. He was more of a listener than a talker, yet everyone liked him and no one ever called him a sissy. My brother, Hal Cullen, was in the same grade with William. He says that William was one of the two brightest boys in the schoolroom, and he still remembers how well William could draw pictures. Hal used to stop by William's home and play after school when he was a boy. William loved to play baseball, and he read a lot, but he did not play cowboy-and-Indian and wrestle much when he was a child.

William used to come to see us at our home in the country. Old Thompson Lake at our farm was a great gathering place for boys. Often he swam and waded in the lake with us and hunted bullfrogs and cottonmouth moccasins with a .22 rifle. He liked to listen to stories I told about hunting, and he asked questions about wild life and little animals and birds. Often we roamed around in the fields and talked about things of that kind. He did not ask too many questions as most young town boys do. He just seemed to enjoy walking around in the woods and observing the things that he saw.

The most distinctive thing about William as a little boy was that he was unusually thoughtful. He was so quiet that his childhood friends do not now remember many things he said or anecdotes about escapades he was involved in as a child. At that time, of course, we never thought that this quiet, dreamy-eyed boy would remember every detail of all he heard and saw and would some day weave these memories into stories and become one of the world's greatest writers.

All the members of the Falkner family that I have known have been fine, gifted people. William Faulkner's grandfather was known here in Oxford as Colonel

Falkner. When I was a boy, I saw and met him many times on the street, yet I never heard him speak. He carried a cane, and he would tap it along as he walked. His walk was peculiar, just like William's. The only other people I have known to walk like that were walking in their sleep. It is not a slow walk, but a kind of mincing step, an odd gait that I cannot describe. No one ever knew what Colonel Falkner was thinking about as he walked. Like his grandson William, he would pass people by and not even notice them. My father and others who knew him well had great respect for the Colonel. He lived here for many years and was buried in Saint Peter's Cemetery in Oxford in 1922.

When I first knew Mr. Murry Falkner, William's father, he and his brother John were in the grocery business on the northeast side of the town square. Later they ran a draying business. Then Mr. Murry owned the old opera house, where the vaudeville shows would put on their acts when they came to town. After that he started a hardware store. My brother and I bought hardware from him on terms. Sometimes we had a hard time paying our bill. When I owed him money, he was very lenient and would give me plenty of time to pay. Later he became comptroller at the University of Mississippi. He was most efficient. He did not have much help, and yet he did almost all the work that a large staff does today. I built part of the football stadium for the University, and he supervised the construction of it. He was prompt and considerate in dealing with all those who worked for him.

I knew Mrs. Maud Butler Falkner, mother of William, from the time I was a little boy. My father knew her from birth. Mrs. Falkner was a gracious, considerate lady who was kind to everyone, no matter who they were or how humble they might be. Although I am no judge of art, I would rate Mrs. Falkner as one of the greatest painters Oxford ever produced. Her paintings are true to life down to the smallest details. The junk called primitive and futuristic art will in my opinion be thrown in the trash where it belongs. I believe that the Falkner boys inherited much of their talent from their mother as well as from their father's family. Mrs. Falkner lived quietly in her home on South Lamar until her death in October, 1960.

I have known John Falkner, or Johnsie, as we old friends call him, all his life. He is a talented man, one of the fastest and most accurate engineers I ever worked under in my long years of construction work. He is a fine draftsman. He spent years with the FBI, came home, tried farming, learned to pilot an airplane, went back to engineering, wrote several books, and went into the chicken broiler business. I have never read any of John's books. I started *Men Working* once, but I did not like it because John wrote about so much filth. Now he paints and exhibits his pictures. He is good painter of rustic scenes. Once he showed me a picture of a possum hunt at night. He is very accurate with his brush, and he had very carefully drawn the firelight gleam and the light falling on the faces of some of the possum hunters. John Falkner has great ability, a fine personality, and many friends. But his one problem is that he has so many talents that he cannot concentrate long enough on any one to succeed.

I knew little about Dean Falkner, the youngest brother. He grew into manhood and was killed in an airplane crash while I was away from Oxford.

The Falkners are reckless. They like thrills and dangers. In the summer of 1959 William broke his collarbone in a fox hunt in Virginia, and then he came home and got hurt again with his jumping horses just a few weeks later. One of them threw him. William is a little old to be fooling with jumping horses. Twenty years ago Johnsie Falkner was talking with me about going in together and buying a cotton-dusting plane. Flying a cotton duster is a dangerous thing, and Johnsie said he would fly it. Dean was killed fooling with an old crate of some kind.

All the Falkners are honorable people. They are honorable, reckless, quiet, and kind.

II

Faulkner and I Grow Up

WHEN I WAS a long-legged, overgrown country boy of fourteen my family sent me to school in town. I was head and shoulders taller than the others in the seventh grade, and the situation was embarrassing to me. But worse than that, my father, who was a good man, had fallen victim to the demon alcohol. Our big family of four boys and three girls was almost destitute.

That year I really tried to learn, and I did make much progress. We did not have uniforms to play football in then, and I tore up my one suit while I was playing football. Soon my clothes were full of patches. When I would ask my teacher to explain anything to me, she spoke sarcastically. But when the children of the elite would ask her something, she was gracious to them. I saw that she held me in contempt because I was poor and ragged, the son of a drunkard who could not pay his debts at that time.

My last day of school was my birthday and Valentine's Day. Our teacher told the class that we would not be allowed to send comic valentines. But graciously she allowed one of the girls the privilege of sending me one of a drunken bum with patched, ragged clothes.

The other children all got several valentines, but that was the only one addressed to me. The class thought it was funny, but I was a badly hurt boy.

That was too much. I quit school and went to work. By the time I was sixteen years old, I was a professional cement finisher. That year I finished fourteen miles of sidewalk in Kosciusko, Mississippi. We did not do much concrete work in the winter. Then I would stay at home and hunt and fish. During the rest of the year I would leave Oxford and work with cement wherever I could get a job. I have tried to live a useful life, but I have often wondered how much more useful I could have been if my teacher had taken a little interest in me and had given me a little encouragement.

After I quit school, I met William Faulkner only occasionally on the streets or at public gatherings. Then World War I came. I went into the army, and William joined the Royal Air Force. For several years I did not see him again.

When Faulkner came back from the war, he had to change trains at Holly Springs, about twenty miles north of Oxford. Somebody told my good friend Walton Miller (we call him Uncle Bud) how Faulkner was standing as still as a statue in the railroad depot. The engineer came by and stopped and looked at him. William was just standing there flat-footed, paying no attention to anybody or anything. He was thinking about something else besides his surroundings. After a while he moved a little, and the engineer remarked, "Damned if it ain't alive." When William heard that remark, he pretended he had not. He never said a word to the engineer, and the engineer never said a word to him. Perhaps this story is not a fact, but it sounds exactly like William.

After he came back from the war, he disgusted a good many people because he wore his British uniform so long. But perhaps that was the best he had at the time. Faulkner never has cared much about clothes. Even today he will dress as ragged as any farmer in the county. For several years he kept a sailboat out at my brother's hog farm and sailed it on the Sardis reservoir. Often he came out to my brother's farm dirty, muddy, and unshaven. He would spend hours in the sailboat and sail it at any time of night.

Faulkner did not court the girls very much, I think, when he came back from the war. Estelle Oldham Franklin had married then, and she was living in Hawaii. Faulkner, I believe, was still in love with her. When Estelle divorced Franklin and came home, probably it was understood that she and Faulkner would marry.

After Faulkner came home from the War, he went to the University for a time, and then he worked at odd jobs. He fired boilers in the University electric power plant for a while. His father was comptroller and got him the job. He worked hard; in those days they had a regular old coal-fired steam boiler. Next he was postmaster at the University. He says himself that he did not get up and wait on the customers. Somebody told a story about how he said he did not wish to be at the beck and call of any son of a bitch with a two-cent stamp. This was in the early twenties. His father was not proud of him in those days. Faulkner would try to work, but to me he looked like a tinkerer instead of a workman. He did not seem to give his mind and attention to work. He did a little carpentry work and was a sort of Jack-of-all-trades. He tried to be a poet and published some poems in the *Mississippian,* the college newspaper at the University of Mississippi. I thought this was a poor way of making a living. Probably he started writing stories almost accidentally. That was what he was cut out for. He tried sign-painting and failed at that, too. Once he was painting a sign for the Standard Oil Service Station, which was built on the corner of old Colonel Falkner's front yard down on South Lamar. He did not know how to scale his letters off and paint that sign. He was stumped, and I did know how to scale letters off; so I did that part of the job for him.

In those days Faulkner would work, but he would also seem to get something else on his mind. He never had much to say to anybody. Those who know him think of him just as an ordinary, likeable man. He is not snobbish; he just seems that way to people who do not know him. He may pass down the other side of the street and not notice a friend. He hunts no one up. Faulkner had only a few friends before he became famous. He will never have many close friends, except for those who are friendly to him now because he is prominent.

III

Faulkner in a Hunters' Camp

FOR ALMOST A century a group of hunters from Oxford and Lafayette County have been going over into the Mississippi Delta for a few days' hunt every fall. I have gone on this hunt for many years. William Faulkner has hunted with us many times, and that is where I have known him best. In my life I have enjoyed nothing more than the annual hunts and my associations with old hunting friends. Most of them are gone now, but to me they will live as long as my memory. In recent years we have owned forty acres and a galvanized-tin camp house on Steel Bayou. Sometimes the weather gets pretty rough, and sometimes the going gets hard. These are the kinds of things that prove what a man is made of. And William Faulkner has proved himself as good a man as ever went in the woods with us. When I first hunted over in the Delta, there were thousands of square miles of virgin forest growing from the rich soil which had come from every state in this great basin and had been scattered by the flooding Mississippi River for untold centuries. In the good old days we had to carry a sharp ax with us when we hunted bears in the big timber of the Mississippi Delta. The trees were so big that two-hundred-pound bears would run into the peckerwood holes when our dogs treed them, and we had to have the ax to cut them out. Leaving the bears in the trees would have discouraged and spoiled our bear dogs.

William Faulkner did not go with our camp when he was a young man. But he did hunt with Colonel Stone's camp even while he was still just a boy, and he killed a deer when he was only fifteen or sixteen years old. Uncle Bud Miller, a member of our camp, also hunted with the Colonel. Lafayette County hunters have always known each other and exchanged yarns. Faulkner's hunting stories are based on our camp and Stone's camp, and he never saw many of the things he has written about. The stories of the old hunters are often the sources of his tales.

I have seen Faulkner doubled up with laughter about predicaments of hunters in our camp. Although he does not laugh often, he can be as merry as anyone I know. He has a merry laugh when he is really amused. He does not pull jokes on other people much, but in his quiet way he will tease some of us old friends—something I do not believe he would do to anyone else in the world. We never pull jokes on him. Even though Faulkner has written some very frank passages in his novels, he never tells dirty stories. When other people tell off-color jokes, he has nothing to say. When the conversation gets too filthy, often he takes a walk or wanders off and sits on a log.

Faulkner is never gloomy. He is always cheerful, quiet, and willing to do his part of the hardest, dirtiest work in camp. I have never heard him grumble about any hardships we ever had, and sometimes it has been pretty rough in the Delta. There was a time when we spent a half a day riding through the woods with a team of mules and a light load. Bogging up to the axles, we could hardly move. As a woodsman, Faulkner is as good as any of us. If he is on a stand, he stays there until it is time to go in to camp. He is as good with a compass as anyone I know. In five thousand acres a man must have a compass to avoid getting lost. When no one will go with Faulkner, he takes his flashlight and goes coon hunting by himself at twelve o'clock at night in the lonely bottoms. Sometimes he rides down the river in a boat at night and shoots coons along the bank as they feed on clams. William has good judgment, and he usually looks at a map before he goes hunting in a new place. There are people yet who are like Ike McCaslin and who can know the Big Woods without using a compass. But people who have spent as much time in civilization as Faulkner and I have must rely on a compass for direction.

Faulkner is a gentle man. He never curses, and I have heard him say that he objects to too much cursing in camp. He is, I think, a religious man, though not a good church man. His actions and the way he lives indicate that he believes in a Great Creator. Faulkner certainly treats people as a Christian would, and he stands for things a Christian stands for. I have never heard him talk about religious things, but of course he is quiet. He does not talk about personal things.

Sometimes Faulkner tells a story about some old person or something that happened in the old times. He does not invent any tales in camp. He tells a story fairly well, but some of the hunters are better storytellers than he is. His tales are not as plain as those which some of the rest of us tell. He enjoys a little depth in the stories he tells. Some of them may be so deep that some of the hunters fail to see the point, but they laugh anyway. We laugh at almost anything down in the Delta.

In camp Faulkner never mentions the books he writes. As long as I have known him, he has never talked about his own business or books or writing or anything of that sort. He never takes to the camp any books to read. Sometimes he reads newspapers or something he finds lying around. When others are playing poker, Faulkner may sit around the campfire and smoke his pipe. If he can get someone to tell him a story, he will listen and smile a little. But always he does more listening than talking. After a drink or two, he talks a little more, but not much. He spends much of his time planning the hunt for the next day.

We have had few drunks in our camp. In the old days Dr. A. C. Bramlett was head of the camp, and he did not allow much drinking or any gambling. Most of the members are hard-working men who are sensible and know that getting drunk is no fun. We all like a few social drinks around camp, and sometimes during hardships we believe a drink is almost necessary, but we will not put up with drunks.

Once we did not have enough trucks going down to the Bottom, and Uncle Bud Miller and William had to ride in the back of Lucky Pettis' pickup in the rain. We always left Oxford about twelve o'clock at night in order to get the camp set up before the next night. Uncle Bud had three fifths of whisky in the bedclothes boxes. After breakfast it was still raining, and William said, "Walton, hadn't we better open one of those fifths?"

Uncle Bud agreed, and that made everything seem fine. They sipped it along and sipped it along, and it kept raining. In order to forget the discouraging rain, they drank all the fifth. Down in the bottoms on the Mississippi levee, Lucky Pettis took the wrong road. He went down the levee and stopped in a mud-hole, and they had to back out. Uncle Bud and William were feeling pretty good in spite of the cold rainy ride in the back of the truck. "William," Uncle Bud said, "they're headed back towards Oxford."

And William said, "Open that other fifth."

On Faulkner's first hunt with our old bunch he did drink to excess. I was not along on that hunt. They were camped on the Sunflower River, about two miles down the river from Bernard's Camp. When Uncle Bud came in from one of the morning hunts, the Negro cook rushed to him and told him that he had better see about Mr. Faulkner. Uncle Bud found him as white as cotton; his eyes were walled back in their sockets, and Uncle Bud saw at once that he was a very sick man. Faulkner's kidneys were locked. The hunters were anxious to get him to a doctor at once, but they were in great distress because they saw no way to do so immediately. Great was their joy when a motorboat from Bernard's Camp came around the bend on the Sunflower River. While they were moving Faulkner to the boat, his kidneys acted and this gave him some relief. He was rushed to the Oxford Hospital, where Dr. John Culley told them that they were just in time, that in a few hours it would have been too late.

Faulkner apologized to our old camp boss for the trouble he had caused, said that he wanted to go on the hunt next season, and promised that it would never happen again. Although I have been in camp with Faulkner many days since that time, I have never seen him intoxicated. He has taken social drinks, but not enough to make him drunk. Stories have been told in gossip and in print about Faulkner's excessive drinking, but many of them are exaggerations or falsehoods. Usually Faulkner can control his drinking, take it or leave it alone.

IV

The Nobel Prize in a Hunters' Camp

ONE OF OUR most memorable hunting years came when we were camped on Cypress Lake between Mc-Can and Hog Bayou in Sharkey County. To reach this camp we had traveled by boat two miles down the Sunflower River and had used a team of mules to pull a wagon four miles through the mud to our camp site. It took all day to go six miles. Even after going to all that trouble to get back into virgin territory, our hunt was not very successful. About all we had bagged was a few black squirrels for our camp pot. After a hard day's hunting and scouting, I came into camp and found that someone had brought a newspaper to camp with the news that William Faulkner had been awarded the Nobel Prize for literature. Mr. Ike Roberts said that William was wiping dishes when the news came and that he never lost a stroke, but continued until the job was finished. Often William is just that unperturbed.

All of us were happy to know that our hunting friend had won this coveted prize. That night we celebrated with a big coon and collards supper. This is one of William's favorite dishes; he would eat coon and collards for breakfast. Then the jug was passed around several times, and some of us took big swallows. Finally we decided that we had had enough and began retiring to our cots in the tent. A big pot of squirrels was simmering and getting tender sitting on some coals near the campfire. Uncle Ike Roberts, our oldest member and camp boss, had promised to make us a delicious stew the following day. I warned our Negro cooks that they had better take this pot into the cook tent before they went to bed, or the dogs would get into it after it cooled off, as they had on previous hunts. They forgot my warning; so our dogs also had a celebration. The next day I was proud that the dogs had not been able to eat all of this stew, but had left us about a third of the squirrels in the bottom of the pot. These we had for breakfast about two o'clock that afternoon.

After I retired to my bed that night, I could hear William Faulkner and his old friend Jimmy Harkins talking at the camp fire. Jimmy is in the air force, and he thought that his commander would let him fly William over to Sweden to get the Nobel Prize. At short intervals Rinsy, William's Negro hired hand who was very solicitous about our comfort and who had the key to Faulkner's whisky box, would come to our beds and ask us if we did not need another little nightcap before we went to sleep. I suspect that some of us had more little nightcaps than we needed. The last thing that I remember before I slept that night was Jimmy Harkins saying he was so-o-o-o happy because he was going to fly Faulkner over to Sweden.

Some of us were not so happy. When morning came the ground was covered with snow and sleet.

The wood was all wet. The dogs treed one cook asleep under a snow bank. Rinsy was asleep with his mouth open in the wagon, and the snow was falling in it. It was a dismal day in a dismal swamp. Yet not a man made a complaint. It was the middle of the day before we could get things dried out and the stove hot. We had breakfast and dinner about two o'clock that day. The next day we broke camp and returned to Oxford. Although Jimmy Harkins did not get to fly him over there, William Faulkner and his daughter, Jill, did fly to Sweden, where he was awarded the Nobel Prize.

A picture of William accepting this great prize from the King came out in the morning papers, and I could not resist the temptation to tease Faulkner a little. In the spirit of fun and horseplay, I wrote the King a letter inviting him to come to Mississippi and hunt and have a coon and collards dinner with us. I have the utmost respect for the Swedish king and his people, and I had no intention of ever sending this letter, but I showed it to our county attorney, who is a great friend of mine. Bramlett Roberts laughed until tears were in his eyes. He called Moon Mullins, of the Oxford *Eagle,* on the phone and told him about the letter. The next morning the story came out in the Associated Press and on the news broadcasts. Then we had to send the King an invitation. I do not know what I would have done if Bramlett Roberts had not helped me rewrite the letter, because I am not used to writing kings.

My joke had gotten me in another jam. Bramlett toned my letter down, made it more respectful, and we mailed it on to the King.

Oxford, Mississippi
December 13, 1950

King Gustav VI of Sweden
Stockholm, Sweden

Your Majesty:

I saw a picture of you giving William Faulkner a prize last Monday, and I'll bet William didn't tell you what a big coon and collards eater he is. Now, I told William to carry some delicious coon and collards to you. If he had I am sure you would have given him a larger prize.

In spite of William's dereliction in this respect, I am sure you liked him, because he is the kindest and most courteous person I ever knew. Knowing this, I am sure he treated you with royal respect and courtesy.

I want to tell you a little secret though about William. He is sometimes incorrigible; he doesn't do everything I tell him to do. Proof of this was found on our most recent deer hunt when I was head dishwasher. (Incidentally, this mastery of mine over William on that occasion convinces me that oftentimes I am greater than he is.) William disobeyed me then; he wanted to get the dishes cleaner than I did and took too much time at that job. It is said, although I don't believe it, that William volunteered for this chore because he didn't want to eat from the dishes I washed. His disobedience did not provoke me to action, although I am twice as large as William, for I remembered that when we were boys he never jumped on anybody his size but always picked out a man-mountain.

Since you have been so nice to our friend, Mr. Ike Roberts and I and all the rest of the boys invite you to our camp next Fall for a coon and collard dinner, for if you are a friend of William Faulkner's you are a friend of ours. This includes the cooks, the horses and the hounds.

Now, King, I want you to be sure to come to our camp
next Fall because I am sure that when you leave you
will say you never had a better time and was never in
better company.

Please be assured that we Mississippians, and particu-
larly we Lafayette Countians, are deeply grateful to Your
Majesty for the courtesies extended our great fellow-
citizen.

Sincerely yours,
JOHN CULLEN

His Majesty proved himself a good sport and took
the joke as it was intended and wrote me the following
letter, which I still have and treasure very much.

Stockholm 23rd December 1950.

Mr. John Cullen
Oxford, Mississippi

Dear Mr. Cullen,

H. M. the King of Sweden has read your letter about
Mr. Faulkner with great pleasure. As His Majesty does
not ride nor shoot, I am afraid he will not enjoy your
planned deer hunting party in Mississippi, but sends you
nevertheless His thanks for your kind thought and His
best wishes for the new year.

Yours faithfully,
ERIK SJÖQVIST
His Majesty's Private
Secretary

Although we sincerely regretted that the King
could not come, I guess it was just as well that he did
not. It is doubtful that I could have taught some of
the members of our camp the proper etiquette for
associating with His Majesty. Despite all I could have
told them, some of them might have been calling him

Gussie before the hunt was over, such as Big Red Bright, who is one of my best friends. We have carried on a verbal feud ever since we started hunting together. One of the big reasons for this has been that, like William, Big Red will not take my advice or do what I tell him to do. Had he done so I might have have made him famous, and I may do it yet despite his lack of cooperation.

For many years when the first frost turns the leaves to red and gold, we have had a supper and get-together to plan our annual deer hunt over in the Delta. When I received my card telling me when and where this supper would be held the year after William won the Nobel Prize, it occurred to me that I could have some fun out of the boys by faking a letter purported to be from King Gustav and saying that he had reconsidered and decided to accept my invitation and was coming over for the hunt and that he had instructed the Swedish Embassy in Washington to make proper arrangements with us for this hunt. My story was that, because he was not used to hunting in wild country, the Embassy, of course, had asked us to arrange to furnish him a big strong man as a guide, bodyguard, and chambermaid.

After reading this letter to them, I made a little talk to the boys, telling them that it was up to us to treat the King nice and see that he had a good time. I told them I had written the Swedish Embassy recommending Big Red Bright for the King's bodyguard and chambermaid. This, I said, would be a great honor for Big Red. Being the King's bodyguard might have been all right, but that chambermaid part got just what I expected from past experience. Big Red was suspicious that I was trying to put something over

on him, and he blew his top.   He wanted to know
what the hell I had done that for; he said that he
was going to hunt and be damned if he was going to
be chambermaid for the King or anybody else.

As William Faulkner was away from Oxford at
that time, he missed that fun.   At any rate I feel sure
that had the King really come we would have showed
every courtesy possible.   If the King had been with
us the night after we learned that William Faulkner
had been awarded the Nobel Prize, he would have had
a mighty fine time, although he might have had a
headache the next morning.

V

Old Times in the Delta

OUR OLD HUNTING grounds in the Mississippi Delta provided a wonderful background for some of William Faulkner's stories. There never was and never again will be on this earth such a paradise for hunting dogs and men as the miles and miles of great virgin forests and jungles of the Big Bottoms. This country has changed. It has been civilized. Like youth, the wilderness has gone, never to return. The men with whom Faulkner has hunted are pleased that he has written about the stories told around our campfires.

Very few people lived in the Delta in the old days. Before the times of deep wells and pure water, it was a dangerous, unhealthful place to live. It was called "the wilderness." To a man lost in those great cane-brakes and thickets on a cloudy day with night coming on, it was a dismal, bewildering wilderness. A man did not have to be a tenderfoot to get lost. I never met a woodsman who was so good that he did not sometimes lose his bearings in that rough country.

For untold centuries the Cold Water, Tallahatchie, Yocona, and Yellow Busha rivers had been flowing out of the hills of north Mississippi. During floods and high water they left their beds and deposited their overloads of soil along their courses. This part of the Delta became higher than the surrounding area, and the streams broke out of their banks and changed their courses, leaving their old beds and channels to form lakes and bayous. Great forests of many species grew from this rich, well-watered soil. And some of the trees always produced nuts and fruit to feed the teeming wild life.

Squirrels by the millions and wild turkeys by the thousands lived in these forests; beavers, otters, coon, bobcat, and mink were plentiful. Timber wolves and panthers lived off the smaller game. But mainly we went to the Delta to hunt deer and bear. Most of this area was covered with thousands of square miles of open woods, where the great groves of older trees had smothered out the undergrowth. Tall grass grew under the trees, forming deer pastures. Surrounding the open woods and running through them were canebrakes and thickets, some small, some several miles in length and width.

These canebrakes, thickets, or jungles were refuges for wild life, and often the best of hunters with the best packs of dogs failed to bag the game they were after in that rugged country. Even the late Paul Rainey with his almost unlimited resources and his great packs of bear dogs often failed. There never was and never again will be a finer hunting ground for sportsmen and great hunting dogs. I have always been proud that Rainey took his famous pack of bear dogs to Africa and that they were the first and only dogs in history to pull down a grown lion.

On one of those bear hunts in the old days we camped close to Rainey. He had the reputation of an autocrat, but judging by the way he treated us, he was one of the finest and most courteous sportsmen who ever hunted in the Delta. Except for old Dr. A. C. Bramlett, all of us were farmers and workingmen. In those days we did not have any dogs. Rainey told us where he would drive and that we were welcome to have any bear we killed in front of his dogs. All he wanted was to know about it so that he could enter it on his records. Few rich men would have been so kind to us farmers and workingmen.

True: The Man's Magazine published an article about Paul Rainey in October, 1957. It does not include an account of Rainey's bear hunting in the canebrakes of Mississippi. Rainey and Colonel Stone had a club house over in Panola County on section 16. As this article indicates, Rainey cared nothing for the meat or trophies. All he wanted was the thrill of the chase. If anyone could beat him to the kill they were welcome to do so; he did not want or ask any odds in his favor.

Many hunters have killed much more game than the men in our camp, but few have had more fun or enjoyed being together more than we have. Of all the men with whom I first hunted in the Delta, Uncle Bud Miller is the only one still alive. All the rest are gone. On my first hunt, old Dr. A. C. Bramlett sent Uncle Bud Miller and Joe Butler, two of our best woodsmen and hunters, to what was known as Brown's Deadening to see if old Reel Foot was still there. Faulkner says that he had in mind this famous old bear when he wrote the story about Old Ben in "The Bear."[1] Old Reel Foot had lost two of the toes off his left front paw; Joe measured his tracks, and they were

1. Cynthia Grenier, "The Art of Fiction: An Interview with William Faulkner—September, 1955," *Accent*, XVI (Summer, 1956), 167-77.

eight inches wide. For twenty years, Old Doc said, he had lived in this jungle, which had sprung up after fire swept through the area and killed all the timber. Thickets of vines and cane grew there, and when the dead trees fell into the tangle it became impossible for man to penetrate it with any speed. Old Reel Foot had either whipped or killed every pack of dogs that followed him into his jungle lair. On my first hunting trip there, a pack of twenty-seven dogs followed Old Reel Foot into the thicket, and only two of them came out alive. How he killed so many dogs so quickly I will never know.

Adjoining this jungle was another strip of country called the Cyclone. Here for a length of about thirty miles and a width of about five miles a cyclone had blown down all the timber. Canes and vines grew so thick in the fallen trees and formed such a tangled mass that a man could get through it only by crawling. These canebrakes and jungles formed a refuge for the many bears who lived in this area. Although I did not realize it then, I saw the beginning of the end of bear hunting in Mississippi. In the fall of 1914 there had been very little rain, and everything was as dry as tinder. While we were on our annual hunt, fires raged through these jungles, leaving them cleaned up and ready to plow. With both food and cover gone there was only one thing that the bears could do—migrate. And most of them did. Then I left the state and spent one year out West and three in the army during World War I. When I returned, the great hunting grounds I had remembered were gone. Towns and cotton fields had taken their place. Today, about all that is left is a little scrubby timber on overflow lands. We have often wondered what became of Old Reel

Foot after his home was destroyed. I hope that this resourceful old rascal did migrate, find a good home, and die of old age.

Never again will man hear the music of such sweet-toned packs of old-time black-and-tan hounds, blue ticks, and red-boned hounds ring through those wild, untamed wildernesses. They are gone. The Indians hoped to go to a happy hunting ground after life here on earth. I too would really want to go to heaven if I thought it would be a hunter's paradise like the Delta in the old days and if I would have my youth and strength once more and be back in camp with the same old friends and companions. They did not always tell the truth, but I would not want that to be one of the requirements to enter paradise. Personally, I would not care much about waking up in a beautiful city with streets paved in pure gold, or playing on a golden harp. I would gladly settle to awake back in a tent in the big woods with my old hunting pals, smell venison broiling over coals and wood smoke, and hear Uncle Ad Bush, our old ex-slave Negro cook, beating a tin pan and chanting in his soft voice, "Raaise up, raaise up, raaise up, bullies, and get yo fower-clock coffee."

In Old Reel Foot's days a man could travel for miles under the open timber and never see a road. Old Colonel Stone owned a good bit of land, the place where he built his camp and the Porter farm, four or five hundred acres with timber on it. He let the Porter farm go rather than pay his drainage tax on it. The Carrier Lumber Company or Lamb Fish, a big-time lumberman, cut the timber and sold the land to people who started farming. In 1915 and 1916 near Charleston, Mississippi, there were miles of lumber in

stacks high as a man could make them. Now levees
and farms have replaced the timber, and where the
game was there are fields of cotton, corn, and soybeans
and pastures. Even though this is progress and even
though it is wise to graze thousands of cattle on land
that once produced only a few wild deer, I am sad
because this period has come to an end. The day
of the bear hunter is over, and the day of the deer
hunter soon will be ended. Now I think each season
is going to be the last one for me.

William Faulkner loves to hunt with men who love
the woods and wild life. He likes to camp with a few
good fellows in a tent. We are confident that it was
around our campfire that he got the background for
his story of Ike McCaslin and the bear. And this story
expresses better than anyone else ever could the great
sadness of change and the terrible sorrow of the loss
of the wilderness.

VI

The Old Hunters

MOST OF THE men of our old hunting camp have not read many of William Faulkner's stories and novels. Our friendship with him is based on the kind of man we have found him to be in our association and camping with him. I doubt that he has any more loyal friends than we are. Faulkner has proved himself to be a good hunter and one of the fairest and most agreeable men we ever had in our camp. Looking back after years of hunting and camping with these men, I find that the kills I have made mean little to me. But the friendships and experiences we have shared are the things I cherish. Some of the happiest times of my life have been spent with these men. Perhaps a few true stories about my hunting friends and Faulkner's will show what kind of men they were and are.

I first hunted in the Delta with that grand old man, Dr. A. C. Bramlett. I remember many stories about Old Doc. On one hunt, we were camped on Stoval Bayou, just east of the Cyclone. We were having a good hunt and finding plenty of game; and Bob Harkins had killed a fine big fat bear. Old Doc invited Governor Brewer and some of our highest state officials to come to our camp for Thanksgiving dinner with us. We drove four poles into the ground and made a table by turning a wagon-bed upside down. Upon this table old Ad, our Negro cook, spread a fine tablecloth and covered it with hot steaming dishes containing bear, deer, turkey, quail, duck, squirrel, fish, and even rabbit and possum.

When the governor and his friends arrived, Old Doc called us all out, including the cook and the woodchopper, and lined us up and introduced us to the governor and his friends. He called us his boys and told the governor we were the boys who had made that dinner possible. Then Old Doc asked the blessing and gave thanks for the blessings God had bestowed upon us Americans. Old Doc meant that prayer. After dinner, the governor thanked us and said that he had been to many fine banquets, but that he never had eaten such fine food.

Once when Uncle Ike Roberts was the head of the camp, we had pitched our tent on a small knoll west of Bobo Bayou. Game signs were plentiful around us; but before we were able to hunt any, it began raining cats and frogs. Soon the water was knee deep all around us for miles. We were in a hell of a mess —how we were going to get out of there was a problem. It rained for three days and nights, and by that time most of us knew how to sympathize with old Noah. Since we had expected to kill game for part of our food, we were running out of groceries. On the third afternoon it quit raining. By wading we could get to a high piece of ground which was not under water.

Mr. Ike said to me, "John, you got any dogs that will tree possums?"

"Yes," I said, "I have some good possum dogs."

"All right," he said, "we will go possum hunting tonight."

When dark came we started out and by ten o'clock that night we returned to camp with a sack full of big fat papaw- and persimmon-fed possums, which we dressed so that Ad could cook them for breakfast. It was damp and cold, and most of our bedding was wet. Mr. Ike had gone into the Negro cooks' tent and slept with them because they had kept their bedding dry.

Next morning, some of the boys did not like the idea of eating possum, and Ike began to laugh. When you heard him laugh, there was something about it that was infectious; you too felt like laughing. I will never forget how he looked, laughing with possum grease running down his chin from both corners of his mouth. He remarked that anybody that could not eat possum for breakfast and sleep with a Negro did not have any business on a hunt. And he roared some more. I had been feeling pretty bad, but I laughed until I hurt. Doing and saying such things at such times proved Uncle Ike's good qualities. He was the man who cooked the coon and collards supper the night after we learned that William Faulkner had been awarded the Nobel Prize.

Uncle Bob Evans, another of the old hunters, was a big rawboned, ham-handed farmer with horny hands and a lot of dry wit. None of us ever got the best of Uncle Bob in a joke, though we often tried. One morning Uncle Bob, Uncle Bud Miller, and William Faulkner were on stands close to each other. The deer dogs had gone out of hearing. The three hunters had gotten together and were about ready to give up and return to camp for dinner when they heard the hounds coming toward them. They were standing beside a nice glade, and William said, "Yonder he comes. Let's get him."

On came the fine buck at a nice smooth lope. Both Uncle Bud and William fired and missed. Why they missed, neither of them could understand, but they never ruffled a hair as he passed them by. Uncle Bob felt so certain that they would get him that he did not raise his gun.

When they came to camp and were talking about it, someone asked Uncle Bob why he didn't shoot and wanted to know what was the matter with him. He fixed Uncle Bud and William as he drawled slowly, "Waal, I don't see what you want to criticize me for. I guess I came about as near killing him as William and Walton did."

Once William Faulkner got a shot at a deer but did not say whether it was an easy shot or a hard one. All he had to say when I asked him if he saw a deer was, "Yes, I got a shot." Since he did not bring the deer to camp, I took it for granted that he must have missed it. Had this been any of the other hunters, they would have explained in detail why they failed to kill the deer. But William Faulkner never explains very much.

Bob Harkins was a farmer, ginner, miller, and a fine man and hunter. Once he had troubles while hunting in the Cyclone. It was said that a man could not go through that jungle of blown-down trees, tall blue cane, and tangled vines; but Bob proved it could be done. One morning I heard a pack of hounds in the jungle. Never having heard dogs run a bear before, I could not figure out for a time what they were after. Then it dawned upon me that they were running a bear; so I found a fairly thin place and entered the jungle. The cane was so dense and had such heavy foliage and it was so dark under it that I could not see ten feet from me. All that day I tried to get a shot at the bear. Finally just before night the bear ran through the thicket so close to me that the pack of dogs around him passed on both sides of me. I was down on my knees trying to see him as he passed, but I could not see him. Before he had gone a hundred yards I heard a rifle crack. Then everything was quiet. Disgusted at my luck, I started to walk away, never dreaming that it could be anyone from our camp. Then I decided to go by and look at the bear. Never will anyone be happier to see me than was Bob Harkins—five miles from camp in a canebrake all alone with a big dead bear and night coming on fast. Bob had torn his clothes into tatters, but we had proved that we could hunt in the Cyclone, and Bob had killed the bear.

Joe Butler was one of the finest shots I ever saw. Just at dark one night Joe shot a bear when it was too dark for him to see his sights. The bear ran into the canebrake, but from the blood Joe saw he felt confident that the bear could be found the next day. Early in the morning, Joe, Uncle Bud, old Doc Bramlett, and Sam Hickman (a Negro riding a mule) crossed a small bayou and found the dead bear a short distance out in the thicket. They hacked a path through the cane to get the bear out, but neither Sam nor his mule would come out in the canebrake. Both Uncle Bud and Joe were strong young men then; so they decided they could tote the bear out. They put the front end of the bear on Uncle Bud's back with its front legs over his shoulders. As they were making their way slowly out of the thicket and were about to wade the bayou, Joe said, "Walton, I've done about everything else, but this is the first time I ever kissed a bear's ass.''

Uncle Bud laughed so much that he let the bear fall in the bayou. At last Sam saw that the bear was dead, and he helped them get it out of the bayou and onto the mule—against its wishes.

Uncle Bud Miller, or Walton as the old timers called him, has been a farmer and a highway worker. He has gone on every one of our camping trips in the Mississippi bottoms for sixty straight years. A great hunter and woodsman, he has hunted longer and killed more big game than any of us. Uncle Bud always seems to be close at hand when help is needed. Once on Stoval Bayou, I left camp at daybreak. About the middle of the afternoon I met Uncle Bud in the woods on the opposite side of the Cyclone from camp and about five miles away from it. As we walked up the bank of one of the Twin Lakes on our way back towards camp, we heard a dog baying alone up ahead of us. I recognized the dog's voice. In all my hunting, I have never heard another dog roar so loud. The day before, I had seen this dog running with a pack of bear dogs, and I had heard him alone baying in the Cyclone all that night. Now we heard the same dog, still alone, cross Twin Lake up ahead of us and bay out in the Cyclone. When we reached the place where we heard him cross, there were the fresh tracks of a big bear and a big dog. We could hear the dog, now no longer baying, about one hundred yards out in the canebrake. Uncle Bud went around and approached from the opposite side while I waited. I saw the cane tops weaving and heard the dog coming straight to me. But the bear must have scented me, because he never came into the open where I could see him. Instead, he turned back out into the thicket, and again I heard the big dog stopped and baying. I did my best to slip up and shoot that bear. I got close enough to see the dog several times, but each time just before I could get close enough to see the bear he would run off a short distance and stop again. We kept this game up until it was dark, and I decided it was useless to try any more.

That great dog was a very unusual dog. He must have stood thirty inches tall. He was of mixed breed and had the biggest, deepest chest I ever saw on a dog, tapering to the back like a prize English bull-dog's, but he had the long nose and long ears and voice of a great hound. I hated to leave that great dog out there alone baying that bear, but even more I hated to spend the night in the thicket. I climbed a tree hoping I might see the open woods. But I could not. With little hope of anyone hearing me, I whooped.

Uncle Bud answered. "I thought you would be damn big enough fool to still be out there; so I waited."

The great size of that dog, his mixed breed, and his solitary chase of the bear in the wilderness remind me of Lion, the great silent dog in Faulkner's "The Bear." This dog barked, but Lion never would cry on the trail of an animal. Some dogs are silent like that. One of the dogs I own now, Old Jughead, never barks on a trail. During my years of hunting I have seen a good many dogs that ran without making a sound.

Once Uncle Bud and Big Red Bright, who is as big and as strong as a bear, drove a T-model Ford up to a honky-tonk down in the Delta to get liquid refreshments needed in camp. After turning around, Uncle

Bud stopped the motor. But then they heard shots in the building and saw men coming out through the doors and the windows. Not wishing to become involved, they started to leave. Uncle Bud flooded the motor and the car would not start. Big Red got out to give it a push. By this time a man had come to the door of the honky-tonk, and he seemed to be shooting at everything in sight. Big Red did not wish to be delayed. He picked up the back end of the car and began running down the road with it as a child would with a toy wheelbarrow. Every time the man shot after that, Red got faster. Uncle Bud said it was a good thing the man stopped shooting because Red was going so fast that he was afraid he would have lost control if Red had run any faster. Sad to say, they did not bring any refreshments back to our camp.

One night in 1958, after the poker game was over and the lying contest had subsided, I had a talk with my friend Sherman Wardlaw, who is a very scientific man. We discussed such things as how to use a hula-hoop to catch a deer and how to keep the dogs from beating us to the persimmon trees in the morning. His brother Mack solved one of the problems. He suggested that we bore holes in the doors, pull the dogs' tails through the holes, and tie knots in them. This seemed like a sensible solution.

In all his years of hunting Faulkner has killed does only twice, and both of those came at times when we had to have meat in camp. On Cypress Lake once, William shot three times at a deer. It ran off, saw the dogs, and came back. Then he killed it, and it was a doe. When Uncle Bud came to the stand after he heard the shot, William said, "Well, Walton, I killed him. Did I do wrong?"

"No," Uncle Bud said, "everybody else is doing it, and we got to have meat in camp anyhow."

"Well," William said, "I didn't know."

Once William shot at a deer with a 30-30, but the deer did not fall. The driver Billy asked, "Mr. Faulkner, did you hit it?"

"Billy," he said, "I don't know whether I did or not."

Then the dogs jumped another deer and left the trail of the first one. Faulkner had killed that deer, and we found it on the hunt the next day. It had spoiled. It was a three-point buck. On another hunt William shot a deer and cut the end of its heart off, and it ran on into the woods a good many yards before it fell and died.

On a hunt on the Sunflower River the dogs ran right across William's stand. He said, "Don't shoot. The first one's a doe. Don't shoot. The second one's a doe. Don't shoot. Bedamned if the third one ain't a doe." Four men with rifles and shotguns let all three pass by. But other hunters right close to them killed all three does just a short while later.

Before the season opened one year, Big Red Bright and I scouted the area where we had decided to camp and found at least three legal bucks' tracks besides a drove of signs of does and little deer. In order to get into camp and get set for the opening morning, we left Oxford very early in the morning the day before the season opened. Big Red is almost a total abstainer and we were in my pickup; so I let him do the driving. I took a little nip of antifreeze every now and then. As we turned off the paved road a few miles south of Midnight, Mississippi, a white cat crossed the road in front of us. The minute

I saw that white cat I told Red that I would have good luck on that hunt.   He asked why I thought so.   I told him he had seen the white cat, but he wanted to know what that had to do with it.   I told Red I could not understand how anyone could be so dumb as not to know that a white cat crossing the road was bound to bring good luck.   When we reached camp, he told the others what I had said, and they ridiculed me. This antagonized me, and I told them that I had only intended to kill the big buck, but since they had made fun of me I would not let them kill any of those bucks, but would kill all three of them myself.   Within five minutes after daylight on the opening morning, I had the smaller buck.   It had taken three shots to stop him. I had lost my fine old hunting horn, and I could not blow dead-call for help to get my game to camp.   So I waited a while and fired three slow shots, a signal we used when we had no horn and had made a kill.

I lost my horn down at Biloxi during the convention of the Veterans of Foreign Wars.   Soon after I registered at the Buena Vista Hotel, I met Bill Stewart, a good friend whom I met while he was studying law at the University of Mississippi.   He wanted to know why I was wearing my hunting horn slung over my shoulder.   I told him that I was looking for bears and asked him if he had seed any bars around there. He said, yes, he could show me one, and he led me down into the Marine Room.   As we were having a few drinks, a crowd gathered around us and asked me to let them hear me blow my horn.   Being an accommodating person, I blew my horn.   That fat Cajun bartender yelled at me and in a rough voice threatened to throw me out if I blew that thing again. I resented his criticism of my sweet-toned old hunting horn, and I decided to see if he could throw me out. So I put all I had into it and really made the rafters ring with three long blasts. That bartender drew back a glass to throw at me, but changed his mind when I told him to go ahead and throw it and I would break everything in there on him. He began wringing his hands and said, "Please, please, you make me so nervous I can't mixa da drinks."

After he said please, I did not blow the horn any more. But I think the managers of the hotel were afraid I would. I left the horn in my room, trusting a couple of Esaus to guard it, and when I returned to my room my horn was gone, and that pair of Esaus had lipstick prints all over their faces. I believe the management sent those women up there and my friends traded my horn for lipstick. I will never own another horn that I will prize as much as that one.

After I fired those three shots, help came, and we brought the first buck into camp. Since I had killed a deer and Uncle Bud can't walk much any more, the next morning I told him to take my stand and I would take the stand he had had the day before. Shortly after I showed him to the stand, I heard him shoot. When I went to him, I could find no sign that he had hit his deer. So I returned to my stand, and shortly afterward the second buck came by. I stopped him. This made two down and one to go. None of those scoffers at me for recognizing that a white cat crossing my path would bring me good luck had seen a live deer or got a shot. They accused me of missing the big deer three times and then killing the smaller buck with those three shots I fired to signal with. They said that anyone ought to be able to kill two deer with nine shots. I tolerated their teasing for a couple of days. Then I began bragging that I had got nine shots and that I was the only one in the camp that had sense enough to get even one shot. That shut them up.

I did not kill the big buck, although Uncle Bud and Big Red Bright did get scared that I was about to do so. After I had killed the second buck and they helped me get him on the horse, they stood watching me ride toward camp. The hounds jumped a deer and headed straight to me. They saw me stop the horse and sit calmly, waiting to kill the deer when he crossed the glade near me. As the hounds continued straight to me, Uncle Bud exclaimed to Red, "Damn it, that lucky devil is fixing to kill that other buck." As it turned out the dogs had jumped a swamp rabbit; so I did not get to kill that big buck, and I am glad I did not.

This, I believe, was the same old buck that William Faulkner wrote about in "Race at Morning," one of the best hunting stories he ever wrote and a fairly true account of a hunt down on the Sunflower River.[1] The old deer would disappear about the beginning of the hunting season and return to his hide-out just after the season was over, just as William says, and that old buck's tracks were as large as William says they were. Mr. Ernest in the story was really a man named Bernard. He enjoyed the race William described more than any hunter I ever knew enjoyed any race I ever heard of. Bernard was deaf like Mr. Ernest, and each had to have a boy behind him to point which way the dogs were running. He did own an old dog named Eagle. The only difference between the

1. *The Saturday Evening Post*, March 5, 1955, p. 26; reprinted also in Faulkner's *Big Woods*.

race in the story and the one we had is that William may have exaggerated a bit the distance they ran.

At the end of Faulkner's story when they got back to Sunflower River, the dogs were worn out, and the deer was walking along, and the little boy showed Mr. Ernest the twelve-point deer and bawled him out because he did not shoot it. Mr. Ernest explained to the boy that if he had shot him they would never be able to have a race like that again. That part was not what really happened. Bernard ran that deer all day long and got in sight of him two or three times, but he never did get a shot. Faulkner's ending expresses well the spirit and the sentiments of the hunters. What Mr. Ernest says in the story was exactly like Bernard. Anybody who knows Bernard would recognize him in Faulkner's story. The little boy was lifelike, too; he was crazy about hunting. The last time I was in camp on Sunflower, they had made him go to school when he wanted to be hunting. That picture in the *Post* looks like a real picture of the boy, the only real picture among the illustrations.

Faulkner's "The Bear," his best fiction about hunting in the Delta, is based on men and animals and natural settings that he has seen and heard about in stories told in our camp. He never saw Old Reel Foot, I believe, or even his tracks, but he has heard many hunters tell tales about him. Probably he never went hunting with Uncle Ad Bush, but old Ash in "The Bear" is like Uncle Ad, and Simon in "Race at Morning" wakes the hunters with Uncle Ad's call— "Raise up raise up and get yo fo o'clock coffee"—which Faulkner has heard us repeat. Uncle Ad went on one camp with us when he was eighty-five years old.

The story about Boon Hogganbeck's going with Isaac McCaslin to Memphis for whisky is, I believe, a true story from the Stone camp. Faulkner says in an interview in *The Paris Review* that he took Boon from the character of a man who worked for his father. But I never knew a hunter exactly like that, even though I have known Faulkner's father and men who worked for him. An old fellow a little like Boon lived in the bottom, a great big bear-looking type of man, but he was not tall. He had eyes like a wild animal, and he let hair grow all over his face. He went bare-footed, walking around among the rattle-snakes in the bottoms. We never killed anything but he was there to claim part of it. He was just a buzzard after the kill. He had little shoe-button eyes like Boon's and a great red beard. The bottom was a hide-out, a wild hide-out.

Once Big Red Bright, Bill Evans, William Faulkner, and I were all involved in an escapade. Bill, a son of old Uncle Bob, is a dry wit. Big Red, a happy-go-lucky fellow, doesn't have much luck on the hunts because he is so big that the deer see him before he sees them. I think the biggest things Red has killed are a squirrel and a swamp rabbit. Big Red takes the dogs and makes the drives. He would not trade places with an angel in heaven when he is tearing through thickets and swimming bayous with a pack of hounds. When man or animal is sick, Big Red can be as gentle as a mother.

We were camped in a tent in the woods east of Steel Bayou and had not killed any game for the first two days of the hunt. On the morning of the third day, I found where the deer were hiding. Since we had not had a race that morning, I suggested that we go there and make a drive that afternoon. We put the dogs in a pickup truck and drove to the place. After the men had had time to get on stands, the dogs were released; and they struck a trail almost as soon as they were on the ground. In less than fifteen minutes we had killed three deer. Happy over our success, we returned triumphantly to camp. I had again happened to kill a fine buck, hitting him perfectly behind the shoulder as was natural under the circumstances. Everyone I met honored me by asking me to have a drink. I met about six of them, took a big drink each time, and arrived in camp triumphant and happy. Uncle Bud had some corn whisky in a charred keg, and it was about the color of shoe polish. He set a jug of this on the table in front of me. All the other hunters congratulated me and insisted that I join them in a little toddy.

I gave the boys a short two-hour lecture on how to shoot and hunt. Not wanting any of them to fail to hear all I said, I spoke in a loud, oratorical voice. Of course my voice got husky, and I felt it necessary to take another little swallow out of the jug at intervals. Possibly this was a mistake—it handicapped me in giving them instructions on how to shoot a deer. I even forgot to tell Red Bright how to see a deer. I should have known that charcoal might make me drunk. Night came, and I went into the tent. Someone had piled wood in front of the stove, and in the dark tent I did not see it. My feet got tangled up, and I fell over that woodpile, and strange to say when I got up my knees felt weak and wobbly. I remarked that I could not understand what was the matter with my knees.

My good friend Bill Evans said, "I know what's the matter, John. Your knees got drunk when your head did."

Uncle Bud advised me to go to bed, and I did.

After sleeping some time, I awoke and felt that I should get out of the tent and get a little fresh air and relief. Big Red Bright put his arm around me and went with me.

We had cleared away the bushes and vines from in front of the tent. I walked to the edge of this clearing and was standing there when we heard a voice from under the bushes saying, "Hey, Red, remember I am over here."

It was William Faulkner speaking. He sleeps in a sleeping bag outside the tent whenever the weather makes it possible. I am glad he was awake and spoke.

In 1958 Faulkner could not go hunting with us. He wrote that he wanted to do something for the camp and sent thirty dollars to be used to help pay Uncle Bud's expenses and mine. This was a generous act, and we thought Faulkner might be offended if we did not accept it. Finally I decided that sending my part back to him would be the honest thing to do, and he wrote a letter telling me how sorry he was that I had sent the money back because he wanted to think that the money was spent to pay the expenses of a good hunter.

In the letter Faulkner said that he wishes that our deer camp could be what it once was—old-time hunters and the inheritors of the old hunters who have gone on before us. He even wrote that he is still keeping the lease on the camp at Sunflower River in the hope that he and Uncle Bud and Lucky and I can return there and camp in tents again. He would like that better, he says, even if we never killed a deer.

Faulkner has no criticism of the young men we have been hunting with; he says they are good fellows, only he does not like their noise. For three years now Faulkner has not been on the hunt. If he goes again, he will take a tent so that he can sleep out and read and talk. I would much rather hunt with just the old hunters, yet I would not like to hurt the feelings of the young men because I know that in their way they have tried to be nice to us. We like to hunt, sit around the campfire, and talk about old friends and the old days, but they like to engage in rough horseplay and games.

William himself owns a farm with plenty of game, and I control a place surrounded by government forest with plenty of game. We are not big killers; we love our wild life and hate to see it wantonly destroyed. All we want is a little meat for our camp pot, the smell of food and campfire smoke, and the quietude of God's forest. The young people do not see it that way.

Naturally I love my dogs. Perhaps my dogs and I are obsolete in the modern world. They do what they were bred to do. I would not have a hunting dog that will not run game. Times have changed. No longer do we have the same kind of people or the miles and miles of free range. My dogs are mostly prohibited, and I am confining them. They do not understand because they want to do the things they were bred to do, to run and hunt. I am sure they think that we human beings are crazy tyrants, and I am not sure they are all wrong. Old men and running dogs are

out of place in the modern world.   Dogs like this
and men like me are obsolete.   Soon we will be gone
and forgotten, and the ways of the men I have known
and of those in Faulkner's fiction will be no more.

VII

Faulkner and His Neighbors

IN ANSWERS TO reporters and in other interviews, William Faulkner has many times insisted that he is primarily a farmer. He owns a 320-acre farm, the old Joe Parks place, which is located in Beat Two on Highway 30 several miles from Oxford and four or five miles from the county line. On the bottom land he raises corn and hay to feed his stock, but he keeps very little stock on his farm. Mainly he feeds the corn and hay to his two jumping horses, which he keeps at his home in town. The hills of his farm are planted in pine trees. Faulkner and his Negro farm manager, Rinsy, grow no money crops, and apparently the farm is an expense instead of an income. Faulkner is a gentleman-farmer who probably does not make as much money as most gentlemen-farmers. He keeps the farm because he likes the country, because he likes to see things grow and wishes to think of himself as a farmer. For him, farming is actually a hobby.

A hundred yards or so from Rinsy's house on the farm is a little building which Faulkner once called his office and in which he wrote and worked. But now he has moved his office back to town. Faulkner himself helped to build this little building. Rinsy says he worked hard on it for three days. Rinsy and Faulkner also built a barn at Faulkner's home in town, and Rinsy says he is a good concrete worker and a good carpenter. Faulkner does not work around the farm very much. Rinsy says he more or less follows the other workers around instead of working himself.

Once Rinsy got drunk, stayed out all night, and came home the next morning to plow. He just ran the tractor back and forth through the corn without even dropping his middle buster or plow into the ground. Faulkner came out to the field and saw him and called his attention to the fact that the middle buster was doing no work. At that point Rinsy said he thought he would just go to the house and lie down for a while, but Faulkner told him instead to go ahead and drop the plow and get the plowing done. Rinsy says Faulkner taught him not to carouse all night.

Faulkner never tells anyone about the good deeds he does, but he is very kind to neighboring farmers. When he changed from mule farming to a tractor, he instructed Rinsy to sell the mules for money if he could get a fair price; if not, he was to sell them to someone who needed them and never to send them a bill. The mules went to men who needed them. They have never been paid for, and no bill has ever been sent. A drainage canal was needed through the creek bottom. Faulkner's neighbors who also owned land in the bottom were old and poor. Faulkner paid for having dredging done and let them pay him their share when it suited them. By the increase in production it was easy for them to pay. I did not learn this from Faulkner, but from one of the men whom he helped. Similarly, Faulkner has paid for the education of his niece, the daughter of Dean Faulkner, who died in the airplane crash. William is a generous man. As one of my friends says, if you want to buy fifteen dollars worth of henshit, William will put up his five dollars. He may help anyone, but no one else will ever know about it. Probably even his family do not know exactly what he did with the Nobel Prize money.

Faulkner has only one living child, Jill. The first, a boy, died soon after its birth. I have heard stories about how the child might have lived if the local hospital had had an incubator. After that Faulkner gave the hospital an incubator. He was profoundly affected by the death of his first-born child, and it is said that he himself held the child's coffin in his lap as he rode to the cemetery to bury it. Once I was employed to straighten out the copings around the graves in the Faulkner cemetery lot. I asked William's uncle, John Faulkner, whether I should improve the little grave of William's child, and he said, "No, they's no telling what sort of attitude Bill would take toward it." So I didn't touch it.

Some of Faulkner's neighbors dislike him and consider him snobbish, but they misunderstand him. They do not realize that he would be swamped with visitors if he tried to extend a warm welcome to everyone who comes to his home. As a matter of self-preservation, he put up a sign at the entrance to his driveway telling passers-by that his home is private property and asking them to please stay out unless they are invited to come. Faulkner dug up his driveway to prevent interruptions. He takes little part in social affairs, and a good many hostesses resent not being able to use him as a drawing card. Again, they fail to realize that if he should let himself be drawn into the social whirl he would have little time for anything else. Faulkner is a thinker, and he considers social life a waste of his time.

In writing, Faulkner uses many words, but in dealing with people he is a courteous, clear-thinking man who gets to a clear understanding very shortly. He does not spend time with useless palaver; he says what he thinks and goes on his way. Those who hunt with him respect his right to be himself and do not resent his ways. If there is anything we wish to know from him, we ask, get an answer, and let that end it. When we have been planning a hunt or have had some other reason to go to Faulkner's home, he and Mrs. Faulkner have been most cordial. Yet none of the hunters ever presumed to invade his privacy or to invite anyone to go with us. He would never forgive us. We leave the invitations to Faulkner's home to Faulkner. He wants to be courteous to everyone, yet if he tried to entertain all the people who wish to meet him he would have no time to write.

Faulkner knows that he would have starved as a writer if he had had to depend on the people of Oxford to buy his books. Before he became a successful writer, I believe, he worked and suffered a great deal. He knows that his hunting friends would still be his friends if he had never written a line. Most of us are not much interested in literature or Faulkner as a literary man. All we know is that he has proved himself a good hunter, a loyal friend and companion, and a man who would help us in any way he could.

Often Faulkner walks down the street seemingly seeing no one and nothing. He is likely to pass by anyone and fail to speak. This is one of the reasons why some neighbors dislike him and call him a snob.

Yet he does see things; he sees everything. It is as if he were in a strange trance with his head tilted back and no expression in his eyes at all. If someone calls him when he is in one of these dazes, he will stop, turn around, and talk. I never bother him, but just let him pass on by. I have enjoyed watching him freeze up and repel some gushy female who was trying to impress others by knowing Faulkner. He is a master at giving people the cold freeze, but I honestly feel that he is anything but a snob. When he ignores people, he is simply not thinking about them. Prominence makes no difference to Faulkner. He is just as likely to stop and say a few pleasant words to some child, an old person, or even a poor, hungry dog, regardless of race, color, or breed, as he is to stop and talk to our most prominent banker.

One of Faulkner's childhood playmates returned to Oxford after being away for a number of years. He got drunk and went down to where Faulkner was building a fence near his home. Though he was drunk and dirty, Faulkner took him into the house and put him to bed. Because of kindness, he cared for a close friend. Later this same man took an English teacher to visit Faulkner, and Mrs. Faulkner said that he could not see them because he was drinking. Probably that was just an excuse because he did not wish to see them. Faulkner would help any friend who is drunk or in trouble, but he wants no one to impose upon his kindness and privacy. A neighbor who had been a playmate of Faulkner's daughter, Jill, tried to take some of her friends to see him and to show them that she was able to introduce them to Faulkner. But Faulkner refused to meet them. She says that is the only time when she has ever seen him angry.

When Faulkner began writing and publishing stories, people in Lafayette County criticized them and said that he had picked the lowest type of characters when he could have written about fine and noble people. When *Sanctuary* was published, his friends were shocked because, they said, it slandered the South. All the criticism gave the story free publicity, and curiosity and scandal caused many very proper ladies to buy and read *Sanctuary* and other works by Faulkner.

Faulkner knows as well as the rest of us that these sordid stories are read as insults to the people of this community. Thoughtless readers do not understand his books, Mississippi, or the South. Frequently visitors from other parts of the country are surprised to meet good people in our community. They read (or misread) Faulkner's fiction and expect to find only ignorant, immoral ignoramuses around Oxford, or Jefferson as he calls it. But it is hard to tell the simple truth about Faulkner. He is a bit changeable and inconsistent, and I am changeable and inconsistent in my attitudes toward his writings. Human relationships and matters of this kind are too complicated to sum up in one simple way.

Although I like William Faulkner as a man very much, sometimes I deeply resent some of his sordid, exaggerated stories about people in this community. Many of his neighbors believe that he writes novels like *Sanctuary* and those about the Snopeses partly to gain publicity and sell his books. Some of Faulkner's writings are about as popular in his home county as a dead skunk would be in a sleeping bag. When Faulkner wears old ragged clothes, digs holes in his driveway, and walks on the streets with a vacant stare in his eyes, he may be using the same psychology that Diogenes used when he pretended to be looking for an honest man and carried a lantern in the daylight to find him. This was one of the greatest publicity stunts in history. Faulkner knows when not to comment, and when to give an interview or write a letter to an editor about a subject of public interest. He always differs with the general public opinion. He is an individualist, an excellent publicity agent for himself, and a genius.

Most of the people who really know Faulkner like him. Intellectuals have a great admiration for him even though he has little to do with intellectuals. It is generally the neighbors who are not well educated that dislike him and have little respect for him. Yet he has a good many close friends who like him very much as a man, even though many of them have never read a word he has written.

VIII

Faulkner and the Race Question

In November, 1955, William Faulkner made a speech about the racial problem before a mixed gathering of the Southern Historical Association in Memphis, Tennessee. He said among other things, "To live anywhere in the world of A.D. 1955 and be against equality because of race or color, is like living in Alaska and being against snow." In this speech he expressed, I believe, his honest opinion.

At this time Faulkner had only recently returned from a tour of foreign countries sponsored by the State Department. Although he was sincere and what he said may have pleased the State Department, the majority of people in Lafayette County and Mississippi consider the SHA talk a poor speech, poorly timed. It came just after the hysteria generated over the Emmet Till case, which was given much publicity by uninformed, sensation-hunting newspapers. His speech did nothing to create good will and harmony, but much to fan the flames of hate and ill-will. Faulkner did not intend the speech to have this effect, but all men make mistakes, and Faulkner, I sincerely believe, made an honest mistake. All good people agree that all races must stand together if we wish to survive and remain free. It is basically a question, however, of how we stand together.

Much has been written about the mistreatment of poor, humble Negroes by unscrupulous white men of the South. Much of it is true—to our shame, as William Faulkner stated. They have been abused, discriminated against, and defrauded. So were the Indians. Noble Northerners graciously gave the Indians a keg of fire water for Manhattan Island, and I would not be at all surprised if they gave them a few drinks before that trade was made. It is, as Faulkner said, to the white man's shame that such things were done. Much has been written about the loyalty of the Negro people to the whites during the Civil War and ever since then. But too little has been written about the white's kindness to the Negro. More publicity is given to a few acts of violence than to innumerable daily acts of kindness between races.

White people of the old South will bitterly oppose the mixing of the races and integration in public schools by force. The rights of the states to run their educational institutions have been usurped by the politicians on the Supreme Court. The right to choose our associates is just as much one of our freedoms as the right to worship or not to worship as we see fit. The Negroes should have every legal right we have. Mississippi is providing Negro schools as good as the ones for the whites, but nearly everyone in Mississippi believes that segregation is best for the welfare and happiness of all the people.

Mississippians believe in states' rights and hope that our government will not become a judicial dictatorship. The American people are gradually being reg-

imented in many ways. Our children should not be
forced to attend classes and associate with a race they
do not wish to associate with. Here in Oxford there
is little friction between white and colored citizens.
Negroes are allowed to vote when they comply with
the law; many of them do vote and no one seems to
object. Most of the Negroes are courteous people.
Even during my own lifetime the Negro people have
made great progress. There are good and bad in both
races. Most of the Negroes of our country have lived
in the South, and they owe much of their advancement
and culture to the white people of the South, despite
what the agitators and communists say. Although
many unscrupulous white men have mistreated the
poor Negroes and the poor whites and anyone else they
could take advantage of, the great majority of Southerners are still the best friends the Negro people ever
had. Many of us would fight for them rather than see
them abused or mistreated.

As Faulkner says, we already have the snow— black
snow, since he was speaking of Negroes. The best
thing to do is to find the best way to live with it.
The best way to do this is to shut up talking about
it and do it. The Negroes should have their own
schools, their own teachers, their own businesses, and
their own parts of town. Let them live together, and
let the white people do the same. All of us have more
fun that way anyhow. God made us different races of
people, and we will get along better living with our
own kind. Damn the friction caused by Negroes living and trying to live in white neighborhoods. And
whites trying to live with Negroes. We are not the
same kind of people; the first grounds for friendship
between races should be the recognition and tolerance

of differences. Faulkner proves by the way he lives that he firmly believes in his right to choose his associates or to associate with no one if he does not wish to do so. And knowing him as I do, I would say that he would be one of the last of men to throw away the rights which his forefathers and he himself have fought to preserve.

John Faulkner bitterly disagrees with William on the race question. He was almost ready to fight when William made the talk before the mixed gathering in Memphis. Many people here believe that William's writings and speeches on the race question are stronger and more liberal than his personal opinions. In many ways his actions show that he is a segregationist. He is kind to Negroes, but he does not wish his family to associate with them socially. He explained to Uncle Bud Miller that he does not believe that the Negro race should mix socially with the white people. If the South had improved Negro schools earlier, William said, the Supreme Court would never have ruled in favor of integration. In a letter published in the Memphis *Commercial Appeal,* Faulkner admonished the colored people to fight for their equality by being humble and patient.

Although the races live separately, there is a deep and sincere friendship between the white and colored peoples of the South. The Bible says blessed is the peacemaker. Waving the red flag of all their past grievances under the noses of the Negro people and forgetting every good deed that their white friends have done for them is not the way to create peace and good will. As William Faulkner said in his speech at the mixed gathering, we are facing the greatest dangers ever known to mankind. Now while we have a little

time we should do something.   Now is the time for the
brave, honest leadership of our people.   Left alone
without trouble-makers, the white and colored people
can work out their differences peaceably.   We have
been friends too long not to do so. There is no better
answer to the racial problem than peace on earth,
good will to men.

IX

Faulkner's Fiction

I DO NOT UNDERSTAND William Faulkner, and I doubt that anyone else does. He does not, in my opinion, want anyone to know him well. No one is really a close friend to Faulkner; even members of his own family cannot predict how he will react to a person or a situation. As a man and as a writer, he wishes to be reserved, obscure, remote.

When I try to understand some of Faulkner's fiction, I see what he means no better than would a little woodpecker sitting out on a limb and saying, "Treat, treat." Some of Faulkner's writing is so true to life that the reader feels that the events actually happened; again, some of it is so obscure that no one can tell exactly what he means. Some passages sound as if Faulkner and his characters were talking in their sleep. Faulkner wishes to arouse the reader's curiosity, to go beyond the limits of the reader's intelligence. He is a clear-thinking man, and he can clearly reveal his thoughts and tell or write anything. But he does not always wish to be clear; he prefers to puzzle his readers, because he knows that many of his readers wish to be puzzled.

I do not fully understand why Faulkner objects to dirty stories in camp and yet writes dirty stories in his fiction, why he is a moralist as a man and yet writes about such completely immoral people. I have never understood, for example, why Faulkner wrote the story about the sodomy between Ike Snopes and the cow. One possibility, of course, is that he does not write for narrow-minded and primitive people like me and many other citizens of his home county.

Many of Faulkner's stories are extreme exaggerations. He exaggerates the ignorance of the poor whites, the nobility of the Negroes, and the decadence of the aristocrats. Many of his characters are freaks. P. T. Barnum knew how to get people to pay to see his show and his freaks. William Faulkner appeals to the same instinct, but Barnum was a piker compared to Faulkner. Faulkner is a successful writer; he has come from coal monkey in a powerhouse to winner of the Nobel Prize. He knows life and understands humanity, and he knows that there is a little bit of the freak in all of us. Probably he does not himself understand all he creates; some things are clear only to God.

Often I understand Faulkner's sources and the life he is writing about more than the writing itself. He seems to have remembered every old wartime story, every notorious and unusual character in Lafayette County, every casual remark, and all the gossip of a community. It is inconceivable to me that one man can have such an uncanny memory. He has had the ability and the keen mind to look and listen, and to use the most unusual and interesting events in Lafayette County history and life. Faulkner found the facts in the life around him and the words to describe them in a dictionary. How he put the facts and the words together is the mystery of imagination and creation. I cannot attempt to explain Faulkner's writing, but often I can tell where he got his material.

Many of the things Faulkner writes about really happened; others are products of his imagination. Since he is writing fiction and not history, he twists events around to suit his fancy and often builds one unusual character out of the traits of several real persons. In reading his stories, I can remember people who made many of the remarks he uses or people who looked exactly as he describes them. He changes characters as much as Pat Stamper and Flem Snopes would change horses before they traded them. Most of the people in his stories really lived; sometimes he uses several characters to make one. Yet no single character in his fiction is exactly taken from life. Faulkner may describe a real person's appearance but develop a personality exactly opposite from that of the person whose appearance he describes. He tells many stories just as they happened up to a certain point, then uses his imagination to change events and make them suit his purposes. "Spotted Horses," for example, is mostly imagination. When we were boys, however, a man from Texas did ship in a carload of mustangs and sell them in a lot near the old Jeff Cook boardinghouse, which still stands. So far as I know none of them got away or created any excitement. The invented details in this story are absurd. Anyone would know better than to chain a string of wild ponies to a barbed wire as the Texan did in the story. Much less a man from Texas. Guts would have been strung about in short order.

Some of Faulkner's writing is fine reading to sell the Yankees. He should never have written some of his stories. True, they are only stories, but many people think that they are entirely based on facts and that they accurately represent the people of this area. At heart, Faulkner is one of the gentlest, kindest men I ever knew. But as a writer he forgets that some of his readers cannot tell his fiction is exaggerated so greatly that it should not be read as a representative portrait of Mississippi and the South.

Geographical details, scenes, and even buildings in Faulkner's Yoknapatawpha County closely resemble actual places and things Faulkner has known in Lafayette County. Dutch Bend probably suggested Frenchman's Bend. The old county poorhouse is located about two miles south of Oxford on the road to Taylor and Water Valley, and in *The Town* and *Sartoris* Faulkner averages giving the distance correctly—three miles in *Sartoris* and a mile and a half in *The Town*. Faulkner's home is on the Old Taylor Road, and he uses that name in *Sanctuary*.

In *The Town* Gavin Stevens rides out to "Seminary Hill, to eat cheese and crackers and listen to old Mr. Garraway curse Calvin Coolidge. . . ." In Lafayette County, Mr. Galloway once owned the store in College Hill for years. No one ever knew his political views. In *The Town* an "original small inflexible unreconstructible Puritan group, both Baptist and Methodist" founded the community, and a similar group of settlers founded College Hill, but Faulkner changed the denomination from Presbyterian to Baptist and Methodist.

In the short story "Shall Not Perish" a little country boy tells a story about "an old lady born and raised in Jefferson who died rich somewhere in the North and left some money to the town to build a museum with. It was a house like a church, built for nothing else except to hold the pictures she picked out to put in it. . . ." The "old lady" was Miss Mary Buie, who gave to Oxford the Buie Museum, which Faulkner describes in this passage. The only thing changed was that Miss Buie, who was as Faulkner says "born and raised" in Oxford, died in Oxford, too, but she did spend a good bit of her life in Chicago and the North.

Faulkner describes the statue of the Confederate soldier on the Square with even more accurate detail than he did the museum: "The courthouse was of brick too, with stone arches arising amid elms, and among the trees the monument of the Confederate soldier stood, his musket at order arms, shading his carven eyes with his stone hand." The actual statue at our courthouse does not have his musket at order arms, but at a rather informal present arms. Both his hands are on his rifle. Here Faulkner has moved the Confederate soldier at the University of Mississippi to the courthouse and described it exactly. The soldier at the University shades his eyes with one hand and holds his gun at order arms with the other. Why Faulkner swapped soldiers, I do not know, unless he considered the University soldier more unusual and striking. These are but a few details which Faulkner has used. The jail, with its barred front window, brick walls, and big central room for the prisoners guilty of minor crimes, is like the real jail in this county. Faulkner has created Yoknapatawpha County from the cloth of Lafayette County.

In *Sanctuary* there is a careful description of a heaven tree in the yard of the jail in Jefferson: "The last trumpet-shaped bloom had fallen from the heaven tree at the corner of the jail yard. They lay thick, viscid underfoot, sweet and oversweet in the nostrils with a sweetness surfeitive and moribund, and at night now the ragged shadow of full-fledged leaves pulsed upon the barred window in shabby rise and fall." A heaven tree resembles a cottonwood. When it blooms, it is a mass of purple blossoms, and the odor can be smelled for blocks. Such a tree does stand in the yard of the jail in Oxford. Several times in his works Faulkner describes a big ditch in the town of Jefferson. Joe Christmas flees through it when he tries to escape in *Light in August.* One of the most unusual features of the terrain in Oxford is the big ditch, which is close to the schoolhouse and not far from the jail and the square. In the old days it was a hide-out, and many fugitives from the law tried to run through the big ditch, as Joe Christmas did. And just as Faulkner says, some Negro homes were built on the edge of the ditch.

The Unvanquished is one of Faulkner's best works, in my opinion. Much of this book is based on actual happenings during and after the Civil War. No matter what part of the South things happened in, Faulkner describes them as if they occurred in Mississippi. For instance, in Sherman's march through Georgia to the sea, he tore up the railroad, heated the rails on burning crossties, and bent them around trees, but Faulkner places that in Mississippi.

My father told me stories about horse thieves similar to Grumby and those who killed Grandmother Millard. Old John Murrell, for instance, would go into a neighborhood and pretend that he was an evangelist. He would preach, and while he was preaching he would signal to his henchmen which horses to steal. Then he would go home with the people, get into a conversation with them, and find out where they had hidden their money. He would tell them about his money and see if he could get them to tell about theirs. If they did not, he sent some of his henchmen back, and they did not hesitate to murder to get whatever they wanted. He was a cold-blooded murderer. They finally caught him, I believe at Richland, Mississippi, and strung him up. He murdered old people, and I have heard that he murdered an old lady. Perhaps that is the source of William's story of Grandma Millard. I faintly remember a story about an old lady who used forged vouchers to requisition Yankee army mules. I believe that happened near Vicksburg.

During the War, no-good horse thieves took advantage of the situation. They preyed on helpless women and Negroes. There were devilish turncoats in Oxford, Sam Howry and Hirsch Howry and others. They became friends of the carpetbaggers and the Negroes to see if they could feather their own nests at the expense of the prosperous people. In the eighties when the army of occupation left this country, the citizens mobbed more white men than Negroes.

When the War began, many of the plantation owners had a great deal of silver and gold. Of course the hillbillies and people who lived out in the hills did not have such wealth. Cotton brought a high price, and people who were wealthy buried their most precious possessions in gardens and different places when the Yankees came. William could have used a hundred sources of that kind for his story in *The Unvanquished*. I heard stories of women who fought in the War with the men, as Drusilla did. Some of them put on uniforms and served in the army as common soldiers.

Old Man is based on truth, but is exaggerated beyond belief. There were too many dead mules and animals floating around in the flood waters. The water in the story was really too swift and too rough. After a flood, the water never gets as swift as William says it is, except when the Mississippi River falls and the water begins to flow off the land. The water rises slowly. It is not swift and rough at all unless there is a big wind to cause waves.

Most of the place names in Faulkner's fiction are based on actual names of real places in Lafayette County and Mississippi.[1] For instance, Freedman Town, which possibly derives its name from the fact that freed Negroes lived in that area before the Civil War, is the colored residential section in both Oxford and Jefferson. Yoknapatawpha County in Faulkner's fiction gets its name from a river, located in the southern part of Lafayette County, which is usually pronounced Yockny and spelled Yocona and which was once spelled Yoknapatawpha on maps and in county records. Faulkner has invented some names, too, in-

1. Among the real places and names which appear in Faulkner's works are Yalobusha County, the Tallahatchie River, Hurricane or Harrykin Creek, Starkville, Oxford (which Faulkner describes as if it were outside Yoknapatawpha County), the Sardis lake or government reservoir, the penitentiary at Parchman, New Hope Church, the Gayoso Hotel in Memphis, Beard's Mill, the Tippah River or Creek, Inverness, Leland, and Holly Springs. Faulkner mentions the Hickahala River, a name perhaps corrupted from Hicaholahala Creek. Pedlar's Field, Old Town, in the fiction perhaps comes from Pedlar's Field, an old abandoned farm section frequently used by fox hunters; Coon Bridge, from Coontown Bridge across the Tallahatchie; Three Mile Bridge, from Four Mile Branch; Alaschukuna River, from the Skuna River, which was once called the Lusascoona; the Pine Hills, from the Pine Hills in the northeast section of the county; Winterbottom's boardinghouse from Winter's boardinghouse.

cluding, I believe, Ishatawa, Achapalaga, Burtsboro Old Town, Battinburg, Okatoba and Crossman counties, Porterfield, and Mottstown or Mottson. So far as I can tell, he uses no consistent system in inventing names or using real names. Of course there are many invented family names in Faulkner's works; but naturally he has used many actual Lafayette County family names.[1] And often the family names he has invented are close to names of actual persons.

Faulkner's reliance on places and names in his native environment does not mean that he always exactly describes places and people he has known. But this resemblance does prove that the materials of Lafayette County and Oxford are so much a part of Faulkner's fiction that a knowledge of this environment does lead to some knowledge and understanding of Faulkner's works. He does invent and arrange, but never so much that Yoknapatawpha County loses all its resemblance to Lafayette County.

1. Faulkner's works and Lafayette County have the following names in common: Mayor Adams, Allison, Armstid, Best, Bond, Buffaloe, Buford, Bunch, Bundren, Burgess, Carruthers, Connors, Cotton, Crenshaw, De Spain, Dupre, Frazier, Gant, Graham, Grier, Percy Grimm, Grove, Halliday, Hamblett, Hampton, Hightower, Hines, Houston, Hovis, Hewlett or Hulett, Isom, Lamar, Ledbetter, Littlejohn, McCarron, McEachern or McEachin, Meek, Odum, Patterson, Provine, Phil Stone, Shegog, Tubbs, Varner, Vines, Wiley, Wilkins, Winbush, and Wyatt.

X

Miss Emily, Nancy, and Some Other People

Few writers can capture in their writings the flavor of the people's folk-tales. William Faulkner has shown a marvelous ability to see what has happened, to remember the tales he has heard, and to use in his fiction the most interesting aspects of the life he has known. Almost all of his short stories can finally be traced to an origin in colorful local characters and events. In his novels he has created very minor characters taken almost exactly from real models, some characters who are totally invented, and some major characters who are mainly invented but partly taken from actual events and persons. Sometimes he uses sayings and talk he has heard, but gives the speech to a character totally different from the real person who said it.

Miss Emily Grierson's love for Homer Barron in "A Rose for Emily" is partly based on the marriage of Miss Mary Louise Neilson and Captain Jack Hume. "The town," Faulkner writes in the story, "had just let the contracts for paving the sidewalks, and in the summer after her father's death they began the work. The construction company came with niggers and mules and machinery, and a foreman named Homer

Barron, a Yankee—a big, dark, ready man, with a big voice and eyes lighter than his face. The little boys would follow in groups to hear him cuss the niggers, and the niggers singing in time to the rise and fall of picks. Pretty soon he knew everybody in town. Whenever you heard a lot of laughing anywhere about the square, Homer Barron would be in the center of the group."

Captain Jack, a Yankee from New England, worked for the W. G. Lassiter Paving Company, which built streets in Oxford in the 1920's. I worked with him on the streets. Captain Jack had a fine vocabulary of cuss words, which he used expertly, and little boys did follow him around and learn to cuss. Faulkner says there was always a group standing around listening to Homer, and Captain Jack was a great teaser and joker. He is up in the eighties now, but he still tells an interesting tale. Captain Jack began to court Miss Mary Louise Neilson. The name Grierson is similar to Neilson, and we called her Miss Mary instead of Miss Emily. Miss Mary's mother died before I can remember, and her father practically reared her. The Neilson people were among the aristocrats in the county, and they objected to the marriage. Good people predicted that she had blundered and made a mistake. But old Captain Jack proved to be as fine a citizen as any man in the county. He stayed here and took care of Miss Mary in her old age and sickness and death. The main plot in "A Rose for Emily" is totally invented. What Faulkner did in his instance was to make a story out of fears and rumors. He wrote about events that were expected but never actually happened.

In "That Evening Sun" Faulkner wrote about events that actually happened, but left them only expected and dreaded in the story. Nancy was terribly afraid that her husband Jesus would kill her; the murder did not occur in the story. It did in life.

About fifty-nine years ago my brother and some of his friends slipped off from home. While they were walking up the railroad north of Oxford, they met some Negro boys. One of the Negroes, Dave Bowdry, started a fuss. My brother had found a tap lost by the trains, and he had planned to put it on a stick to use as a weapon in rabbit hunting. He became so angry at what Dave said to him that he threw the tap and struck Dave back of the ear, knocking him off the railroad.

Then Dave threw several rocks at my brother. He dodged, and they came to grips. In the scuffle that followed, my brother was tripped. Dave jumped on top of him and began pummeling him in the ribs.

Not being pleased to have anyone sit astraddle of his head and beat him with his fists, my sweet-natured brother got a mouthful of Dave. Dave jumped high and released him, but my brother bit a hole in Dave's pants and some flesh out of Dave. Then he knocked Dave down and beat him. Each time my brother released him, Dave would throw big rocks at him. Finally, after dodging the rocks, my brother beat Dave into a helpless condition and got away, but he never claimed that he had whipped Dave. He said that the only way Dave could be whipped was to kill him.

Dave was a probable source for Jesus, the husband of Nancy in "That Evening Sun." Faulkner's description of Jesus fits Dave. Dave did knock his wife in the head, cut her throat as though butchering a hog, and throw her body behind the bed. He was the Negro who was held in the murderer's cell behind the heaven tree which still stands near the jail, and he sang songs as Faulkner says in *Sanctuary*. He was not hanged or electrocuted, but was sent to the penitentiary at Parchman for life. He was shot and killed by the guards there when he told them to shoot and be damned, he was leaving.

There is a ditch like the one Nancy had to cross behind the place where the Faulkners used to live. Dave committed the murder a short distance from the Faulkner home.

After the crime, the Negroes of the county decided that they would mob the jail, take Dave out, and hang him. All of my family were perfectly willing for them to do so, and we let them borrow all our guns. There were rumors that the authorities would let them have Dave, and I went to see a Negro mob in action. At first they were dispersed by a big deputy sheriff with a long six-shooter in each hand. Again they gathered into a mob and went to the jail and knocked on the back gate of the jail yard. Mr. John Burrow, the jailer, asked who was out there.

Johnny Webb told him, "Dis is Johnny Webb."

Mr. Burrows asked what they wanted.

Johnny told him they wanted "that there nigger out of thar."

Mr. Burrows told him they could not have him and suggested that they come back the next week.

Johnny thanked him politely, and the members of the Negro mob went to their homes.

When Faulkner first created his character V. K. Ratliff, he gave him the name of V. K. Suratt. Later he changed the name to Ratliff, he says, because a sewing-machine salesman named Suratt turned up in the county. But June Suratt turned up long before Faulkner created V. K. Suratt in his fiction, and I am convinced that this famous character was modelled on June Suratt, Lafayette County's most famous trader. June would trade for anything he could make a sharp trade for—land, horses, sewing machines. But mainly he was a sewing-machine salesman. Like Ratliff, he carried his sewing machines around on a buggy. June was honest, but he was a tricky, sharp trader. A man could not trust anybody in a hoss trade in those days. That was an old custom and part of the fun of living. The old saying here was that all was fair in love and war and a hoss trade. People were not expected to tell the truth in a trade. June Suratt was a big talker, always full of fun and jokes.

In *Requiem for a Nun* Faulkner describes "a German private, a blacksmith, a deserter from a Pennsylvania regiment, who appeared in the summer of '64, riding a mule, with (so the tale told later, when his family of daughters had become matriarchs and grandmothers of the town's new aristocracy) for saddle-blanket sheaf on sheaf of virgin and uncut United States banknotes. . . ." This is an old story. The German was old Bully Wohleben (we pronounce it Woolubun), who was with Forrest's regiment. They captured a Federal payroll somewhere between here and Memphis, and old Bully made saddle-blankets out of uncut bills. He brought three horse loads of those Federal banknotes home. He said nothing, quietly ran his blacksmith shop, and bought a lot of land in Texas and a lot of land in Oklahoma. In Texas he owned more land than a man could ride across in a day in any direction. Then when his daughters married, he set all his sons-in-law up in business. When he was an old man, he still ran his blacksmith shop. One of his daughters owned a bedspread made of ten-dollar bills that were never cut apart until a few years ago. When one of old Bully's grandsons died in Oklahoma, his estate was valued at thirty-eight million dollars.

Another short and factual portrait in *Requiem for a Nun* is that of the Negro who was United States marshal during Reconstruction and "who was still living in 1925—fire-maker, sweeper, janitor and furnace-attendant to five or six lawyers and doctors and one of the banks—and still known as 'Mulberry' from the avocation which he had followed before and during and after his incumbency as marshal: peddling illicit whiskey in pint and half-pint bottles from a cache beneath the roots of a big mulberry tree behind the drugstore of his pre-1865 owner. . . ." Mulberry was actually Ad Brown, who was given the name Coconut because he bootlegged whisky in coconuts. There was a Negro named Mulberry here, but he never sold whisky. The description does not fit him—just the name. Old Ad Brown had been marshal here during Reconstruction days, as Faulkner says. He was a big-mouthed, one-legged bully. Once when Ad was marshal an ox-driver drove his wagon beneath the post of a little awning in front of the Colonial Hotel. Ad ran out to arrest him, and the fellow went to work on Ad with his ox-whip. Ad tried to shoot him, but he couldn't. The man cut Ad's clothes all to pieces with the ox-whip. Local citizens collected money and paid his fine for whipping Ad. Ad lived, as Faulkner says, until about 1925. At football and baseball games, he yelled in a loud voice for the home team and sold coconuts. The boys all knew that he had punched the eyes out of the coconuts and filled them with whisky. In "The Bear" Faulkner describes the same man but calls him Sickymo: "a United States marshal in Jefferson who signed his official papers with a crude cross, an ex-slave called Sickymo, not at all because his ex-owner was a doctor and apothecary but because, still a slave, he would steal his master's grain alcohol and dilute it with water and peddle it in pint bottles from a cache beneath the roots of a big sycamore tree behind the drug store. . . ." All the drug stores in Oxford sold whisky for a long time after the Civil War, and many times they had a Negro to do the bootlegging for them.

In several short stories and two novels, Faulkner uses characters named Quick. Uncle Ben, Solon or Lon, and Isham derive at least their last name from the Quick family in Lafayette County. They used to live out in the Woodson Ridge area in the northeast part of the county. Old Ad Quick was a farmer and a miller, and the Quicks in Faulkner's books own a saw mill. Solon Quick in "Shall Not Perish" made his wife pay him from her egg money when she rode to town on Saturday in his school bus-truck. Faulkner probably got the idea for that incident from one of his hunting companions—a man who did treat his wife in just that fashion. Sultan Quick ran for sheriff once and got many votes. He had a rough past, but he joined the church and became very religious. The Baptists backed his political campaign. He said he would never drink any more. After the election the very first thing he did was to get drunk. He did not attend the Baptist Church until he entered the race for sheriff again.

These are some of the characters I have recognized. There are many others. Like Montgomery Ward

Snopes in *The Town,* a photographer here got into trouble by selling lewd pictures.   Simon Shegog, who drove for Judge Silvey, may have suggested to Faulkner the character of old Simon, the driver for the Sartorises.   Ratliff gets involved in a trade for goats in *The Hamlet,* and there have been at least two goat ranches in the county.   In *Go Down, Moses* Faulkner bases a story on celluloid collars.   I never saw one such as he describes with the race between the Natchez and the Robert E. Lee painted on it.   In Faulkner's story a white man sticks matches to the collars of several Negroes.   Somebody was always ready to stick a match to one of those collars as a joke.   They could really get hot.

Every Lafayette County citizen who has read Faulkner's works has recognized some of the things he has written about.   But to document fully all his works, everyone in the county would have to annotate his own copy of every work, and even then the changes would prevent complete recognition.   All the readers and story-tellers in north Mississippi could not explain well Faulkner's way of combining reality and his creative imagination.

XI

The Sound and the Fury and *Sanctuary*

MORE THAN FIFTY YEARS ago I often passed the Falkner and the Oldham children playing along South Lamar Street, which at that time was a wide, quiet, shady street. Invariably I saw a Negro woman standing quietly and watching the children. I never heard her speak a word. She was Caroline (or "Callie") Barr Clark, to whom Faulkner dedicated *Go Down, Moses*. She watched after the Oldham children almost as much as she did the Falkners, and they were constantly together. Perhaps William Faulkner took from her some of the traits of Dilsey, the old Negro who worked for the Compson family in *The Sound and the Fury*.

Years passed. My family moved to Oklahoma. World War I came. I volunteered and spent three years overseas. William Faulkner and Estelle Oldham, his childhood playmate, married. Callie Barr Clark lived with Faulkner and his wife. When she became old, the Faulkners never thought of displacing her for a younger woman. She had been their old mammy when they were little, and they did not forget. After Faulkner became a successful writer, they built old Mammy Callie a private room in their shady yard.

She was a privileged character around their home. Born in slavery, she felt that the family belonged to her.

Faulkner could not have treated his own mother with more kindness and consideration. When hogs were killed on his farm, he instructed his foreman to dress and cut them up and lay them out on a table. Then he drove Mammy Callie out to his farm and let her choose any parts she wanted. Finally at the age of one hundred years, Mammy died in 1940. Everything that could be done for her was done. Her funeral was held in the living room of Faulkner's home, and William himself preached the funeral.

Mammy Callie was buried in Saint Peter's cemetery here in Oxford. On her tombstone is this inscription: "Callie Barr Clark. Born 1840. Died 1940. Beloved by her white children."

Callie Barr Clark is one of the most recognizable sources for *The Sound and the Fury,* but the citizens of Oxford who have read the novel also easily identify the source of Faulkner's portrait of the idiot, Benjy Compson. He was based on Elwin Crandle*,[1] the son of a doctor. Although he lived to be more than thirty, his mind never did develop. Just as Benjy Compson tried to catch a little girl, Elwin Crandle chased little girls and frightened them. There is again more brutality in the fiction than there was in fact: no one actually attempted to solve the problem by castration.

Elwin's cousin and I once caught some possums, and we built a cage for them at the Crandle home. Elwin wore a dress until he was at least twelve years old. As we built the cage, he watched us and played

1. Here and later in this book an asterisk indicates that I have used a fictitious name instead of the real one.

with his testicles all the time. The family had a difficult time keeping him under control. They would
pull his dress down, and they kept him inside the high
fence around their yard. Somebody looked after him
all the time. When the child was born, his parents
were proud of him because he had a fine big head.
Then he developed into an abnormal child, and it
broke their hearts. His father was a fine man, and
Elwin's sisters, unlike Candace Compson, were all
ladies. Dr. Crandle quit practicing medicine after an
unfortunate accident. In the dark, he accidentally
mixed some poison instead of the prescription he intended to and gave it to a lady and killed her. He
said that a man who did a thing like that should quit
practice. He was a fine man, and he was big enough
to admit a terrible mistake.

The Crandles were related to the family of Jacob
Thompson, who was Secretary of the Interior under
President Buchanan, and *Jacob Thompson* as a name
is very close to *Jason Compson*. Elwin's brother is
still living. Like the youngest Jason Compson, he was
in the hardware business—at one time, I think, as the
partner of Faulkner's father. He never married. He
played around with women for a long time, but I
don't believe that he ever consorted with a woman like
Lorraine, Jason's prostitute friend from Memphis.

Faulkner himself, however, has not as a writer been
entirely unacquainted with such women. Sections of
Sanctuary exactly describe the red-light district of
Memphis and some of the people who lived there in
the 1920's. Many middle-aged men who tell stories
about the wilder days of their youth remember a house
of prostitution like the one run by Miss Reba Rivers.
I knew Temple Drake, or a girl a great deal like her

named Una Johnson, and many of the other characters
in *Sanctuary*. In 1924 I met Una in a cafe in Memphis. She must have seen by looking at me that I
was a noble, heroic character, because she let me see
her crying. Since she was such a beautiful girl, I
naturally offered to assist her if I could. She handed
me a little note telling me to come to a certain address
on Adams Avenue that night about eight. She wanted
to talk, she said, but was afraid to do so in the cafe.

In those days I was young and brave and foolish.
At eight o'clock I passed through the latticed porch
that William describes so well and rang the bell. A
Negro maid like Minnie opened the door, and I called
for Una Johnson. Minnie locked the door and ushered
me to a room on the third floor.

Poor Una, there she lay, dressed in very thin
clothes which showed what a beautiful girl she was.
She was crying; so I took her in my arms and comforted
her. Then she told me her story: she was a judge's
daughter from Winona, Mississippi; Senator Snipes's
(not Snopes) son, Hubert, had brought her to Memphis and was forcing her through fear to work for him;
she wanted to go home, but was ashamed; if she could
get away from them, get some decent clothes and the
money to go home on, she would do anything in the
world she could to repay me. I did not say that I
did not care for any pay. Being the generous hero
I was, I gave her the money so that she could buy herself some clothes and go home to her mother.

But she did not go. The low-down pimps, she said,
took the money away from her. I doubted it.

So the next time I gave her the money to go home
on, I was somewhat suspicious. After starting down
the stairs, I turned and silently went back up the stairs

to Una's room.   Inside, I could hear great laughter.
Senator Snipes's son, Hubert, was in the room with
her, and they were laughing about how I had been a
sucker.   When I heard this, I got mad, burst the door
open, and took the money out of Una's hand as she
was handing it to Hubert Snipes.   I told them what
low-down skunks they were.

That was the end of my experience with the
judge's daughter in Memphis.   I do not know whether
she was a judge's daughter or not.   But from William's
description of the characters and the latticed porch,
I would say that he and I met the same girl.

I believe that I know one of the barber's college
students who lived in a whorehouse without knowing
what the place was.   The man I know was naïve
enough to rent a room in a whorehouse like that.   The
Coop, referred to in *Sanctuary,* was the actual nick-
name of the dormitory in which Temple is supposed to
have stayed on the campus of the University of Mississippi.   The bridge between the University and the
town is the same in Faulkner's fiction and in fact.

In one instance two paragraphs of *Sanctuary* are
more accurate than most reporting in newspapers.
Faulkner describes "a negro murderer in the jail, who
had killed his wife. . . .   He would lean in the window
in the evening and sing.   After supper a few negroes
gathered along the fence below—natty, shoddy suits and
sweat-stained overalls shoulder to shoulder—and in
chorus with the murderer, they sang spirituals while
white people slowed and stopped in the leafed darkness that was almost summer, to listen to those who
were sure to die and him who was already dead singing
about heaven and being tired; or perhaps in the intervals between songs a rich, sourceless voice coming

out of the high darkness where the ragged shadow of the heaven-tree which snooded the street lamp at the corner fretted and mourned: 'Fo days mo! Den dey ghy stroy de bes ba'ytone singer in nawth Mississippi!' "[1] Anyone who passed by the jail in Oxford at the right time of day saw this scene, but only a great writer can see as much as Faulkner did and describe it so effectively. Only after I read about it do I remember so clearly the actual Negroes who did stand in front of the jail hanging on the fence in this fashion, Dave Bowdry's singing, and people slowing down or stopping to listen to the darkies sing. Faulkner seldom follows life exactly, but even when he does record the literal truth, he uses his imagination to make the writing poetic, unusual, and detailed.

1. Faulkner has said that he first heard this story told by Roark Bradford, but I believe that probably he took this speech from Bradford's story but placed it in an Oxford setting.

XII

The Yocona River and *As I Lay Dying*

THE YOCONA RIVER, once called the Yoknapatawpha, appears often in Faulkner's fiction; it floods and almost prevents the Bundren family in *As I Lay Dying* from getting to Jefferson and burying Addie Bundren in the cemetery where she wished to be buried. The Yocona heads out of Pontotoc County and drains an area composed of steep hills and valleys and forests in Lafayette County. In my boyhood this was one of my favorite playgrounds. In the old days before a straight channel was cut, the river curved and twisted through virgin forests. Great trees, undermined on its bank by swift water, would fall into the river and across it. Other trees, washed out by the roots, would lodge against them, and dead brush would collect and stop the flow of water. In times of heavy rain the river could not carry off the water from the swift creeks running out of the long narrow valleys coming into the Yocona. Flood waters would cover Yocona bottom from hill to hill, back up into the bottoms of the creeks emptying into the river, and leave a coat of fertile soil on the overflowed ground. Usually there was enough time after the floods to raise crops on the fine soil. But much of the river bottom was virgin forest.

In this way the Yocona River became a long chain of lakes teeming with fish, bullfrogs, turtles, and water moccasins. Some of the happiest times of my life were spent in this bottom, squirrel hunting and fishing during the days and listening to old hounds chase coons at night. Often I sat on a log in Yocona River or Yellow Leaf Creek and took the redbirds' advice to "Fish deep, fish deep" for the big catfish living under the drifts of logs and brush and in the quiet, deep eddies. No place on earth has ever looked so beautiful to me as the banks of these streams shaded by the old beech groves that grew alongside them. It is small wonder to me that Faulkner found in the wooded hills and fields along Yocona River bottom subject matter for his fiction. He is a keen student of nature, and he spent much of his boyhood roaming over the hills and valleys near Yocona.

When I was a little boy, my sister taught school down at the Market School near the Yocona River. One Friday afternoon my brother and I drove a wagon and went to bring her home for the week end. We stopped at a home where a young woman had just died in giving birth to a baby. People were crying. I was a little boy, and I remember that as one of the saddest days of my life. The coffin was home-made, built out of newly sawed boards. The conditions of life for poor people in those days were hard. In *As I Lay Dying* Faulkner well describes poor whites, the way they lived, and some of their customs. Cash's building his mother's coffin while she was still alive, for example, would not have been thought a terrible thing in those days. Some country people built their own coffins before they died.

Perhaps the Hellrod* family provided a vague suggestion of the story of the rotting corpse which Faulkner tells in *As I Lay Dying*. All the members of this distinguished family had one major trait in common: they were born mad at the world and everyone in it, and they stayed that way as long as they lived. If any single one of them ever had a friend, I never knew about it. They fought among themselves and fought everyone they saw. I first saw Al Hellrod when I was a little boy. At the time he was in a chain gang working on our county roads. Time after time in later years, he was arrested and fined for drunkenness, disturbance of the peace, assault and battery, and gambling and fighting with Negroes. To everyone's gratification, most of the time the Negroes won.

Al was tough, though, and getting whipped did not faze him. One night he and Will Browning had a drunken fuss and started to fight in Brooks Patton's barber shop. Brooks told them to get out of his shop if they had to fight. Of course Al paid no attention to the warning, and the roughhouse fight got worse. Brooks burst a cast-iron spittoon on Al's head and pushed him out in the street while he was still dazed. As Al wiped the blood and tobacco juice out of his hair, he told me that Brooks had done him a dirty trick.

Al next distinguished himself by slugging a big guard at the county farm. He ran off with a ball and chain on his leg. A Negro who saw him escape said that when Al passed him the ball and chain were going chuckalucka, chuckalucka, until Al went out of hearing. When Al was caught, he was as happy as a lark, drunk, shooting craps at a Negro picnic. Probably the Negroes called the police because they did not want Al at their party. Al was killed in a fight north of the Tallahatchie River. He left this life as he came into it, fussing and fighting.

Mag Hellrod was Al's sister. Once some boys, some dogs, and I crossed her place while we were rabbit hunting. She cussed us in a loud voice and shot a big pistol over our heads in the tree tops. She was only a blustering bluff, and we continued happily down Toby Tubby Bottom. Mag and her sister entertained the toughest characters in this community, and the parties at her house usually ended up in fights. Once Colonel Stone, who owned land adjoining Mag's place, had a surveyor to run the line. Mag ran the surveyor off, and when the Colonel went out to try to adjust matters, she stuck the barrel of her old forty-five in his stomach and called him an old, bald-headed son-of-a-bitch and told him that he had better not try to steal any of her land. She must have been most pleased when she remembered all the inspired cuss words she had called the old Colonel. Her vocabulary was wonderful.

Mag had a grown son who was born without the public or neighbors knowing who his father was. The son, Ab, must have resembled his father, because he was not nearly so mean as a pure-blooded Hellrod; he was only ignorant, low-down, shiftless, and not worth a damn. Poor old Ab finally found a woman ignorant enough to live with him and call herself his wife. She was a big, lazy, dirty, goofy thing, but she had her good point. She had a great deal of affection for her flock of geese.

Ab died in Sumner, Mississippi, during very hot weather. In some way his wife sent word to old Mag that Ab was dead and that she had no way to get him buried. Old Mag went to Uncle Bud Miller for help, and of course he agreed to let his work go, take his car, go over to Sumner, and bring the body to Oxford for burial. When he arrived, Ab's body was still lying on the bed where he had died, and it stank so bad that Uncle Bud could not soberly stand it. So he bought a pint of whisky, drank it, bought another, and asked an undertaker to help him put the body in a coffin and load it in his car. Ab's wife said she could not leave to go to the funeral because she did not know who would take care of her "gooses."

"To hell with the gooses," Uncle Bud said; "we got to get this man buried. Come on, let's go." But she stayed at home.

Uncle Bud arrived in Oxford at night. The body stank so bad that Uncle Bud and Claud Roach, the undertaker, dug the grave and buried Ab that night.

Uncle Bud has told this story several times in camp. If William Faulkner did not know this story and use it in *As I Lay Dying,* there are still some general similarities. The Bundrens, however, were much better people than the Hellrods.

XIII

Joe Christmas and Nelse Patton

AT NOON ONE day late in August, when I was a boy fourteen or fifteen, my father Linburn Cullen, who was then a deputy sheriff, was called by telephone and told that a Negro had just killed a woman out north of Oxford and that he should come to join a posse at once. Before leaving, my father instructed me and my older brother to stay at home and keep out of trouble. But as soon as he had gone, we picked up our shotguns and headed to the place where we thought the killer would travel as he fled to the nearest big thicket from the location of his crime.

As we drew near this place, we heard gunfire and saw a big Negro run across the railroad at Saddler's Crossing about two hundred yards ahead of us. At that time I could run like a foxhound and I never lost sight of him until he jumped into a vine-covered ditch leading into Toby Tubby Bottom. He was running along a valley between two hills, and my brother ran down one of them and I the other. In the valley there was one clear place which the criminal would have to cross before he reached the big thicket in Toby Tubby Bottom. I kept my eyes on this opening, and when I reached it, I knew that he was hiding somewhere back up the valley. The posse was coming on, so I knew that soon we would have him. When the Negro, Nelse Patton, saw that I knew he was hiding in the thicket, he attempted to come by me. I yelled for him to halt and when he kept on running, I shot at him with squirrel shot from both barrels of my shotgun. This stopped him. But that was about the first time I had ever shot anything bigger than a cottontail rabbit, and my squirrel shot were far too small to do much damage at that distance.

I reloaded and ran up close to him and told him to put up his hands. He said to my brother, "Mr. Jenks, you knows I'se a good nigger."

"I know you're a good nigger," my brother said, "but get your hands up." But Nelse never did put his hands up.

He was still standing up, and I believe he was trying to get a chance to grab my gun. If he had tried this, I was ready to shoot him between the eyes. Mr. Curt Hartsfield, the sheriff, and his deputy, Mr. Guy Taylor, rode up. When Mr. Taylor searched him, he found in his pocket a bloody razor with one corner broken off. I probably would have been killed if my father had not accidentally shot a big forty-five Colt out of Nelse's hand with a long-distance rifle shot as he went over a high hill north of Oxford.

After turning Nelse over to the sheriff, I went to the scene of the crime. Mrs. Mattie McMillan was lying in the dusty road about seventy-five yards from her home. How she had run that far I do not know. Her head had been severed from her body, all but the neck bone. Dr. Young, who was examining her, found sticking in her neck bone a piece of steel which fitted the gap missing from Nelse's razor.

The news spread over the county like wildfire, and that night at least two thousand people gathered around the jail. Judge Roan came out on the porch and made a plea to the crowd that they let the law take its course. Then Senator W. V. Sullivan made a fiery speech, telling the mob that they would be weaklings and cowards to let such a vicious beast live until morning. Mr. Hartsfield, the sheriff, had left town with the keys to the jail, because he knew people would take them away from him. My father was deputized to guard the jail. Had he had the slightest doubt of Nelse's guilt, he would have talked to the mob. If this had not proved successful, they would have entered the jail over his dead body. After Senator Sullivan's speech, the mob began pitching us boys through the jail windows, and no guard in that jail would have dared shoot one of us. Soon a mob was inside. My brother and I held my father, and the sons of the other guards held theirs. They weren't hard to hold anyway. In this way we took over the lower floor of the jail.

From eight o'clock that night until two in the morning the mob worked to cut through the jail walls into the cells with sledge hammers and crowbars. In the walls were one-by-eight boards placed on top of one another and bolted together. The walls were brick on the outside and steel-lined on the inside. When the mob finally got through and broke the lock off the murderer's cell, Nelse had armed himself with a heavy iron coal-shovel handle. From a corner near the door, he fought like a tiger, seriously wounding three men. He was then shot to death and thrown out of the jail. Someone (I don't know who) cut his ears off, scalped him, cut his testicles out, tied a rope around his neck, tied him to a car, and dragged his body around the streets. Then they hanged him to a walnut-tree limb just outside the south entrance to the courthouse. They had torn his clothes off dragging him around, and my father bought a new pair of overalls and put them on him before the next morning.

Nelse Patton's crime and the lynching of Nelse are more widely known than anything else of this kind that ever happened in Lafayette County. William Faulkner was eleven years old at the time, and since he has spent most of his life in this community, he must have heard numerous stories about the Patton case. Faulkner has written about many lynchings in his books, and I believe that several of them are generally based on the story of Nelse Patton.

In some ways, the entire book of *Light in August* is centered around the lynching of Joe Christmas, and it seems to me that Faulkner used the stories he had heard about the Nelse Patton case. There are a number of parallels between the stories of Nelse and Joe. Joanna Burden and Mrs. McMillan both lived outside of town, and each of them had her throat cut from ear to ear by a Negro man using a razor. Nelse and Joe both attempted to escape in a similar way over similar terrain. Both of the Negro men were lynched: Nelse was shot in the jail, and Joe was shot in the kitchen of the Reverend Hightower. Senator Sullivan, who incited the mob to riot in Oxford, reminds me a little of Percy Grimm, who led the lynchers in *Light in August*. Both bodies were mutilated, though in slightly different ways. These likenesses seem more important because Faulkner knew more about Nelse Patton's lynching than about any other single episode of that kind.

In *Sanctuary*, also, Faulkner describes almost exactly Nelse Patton's murder of Mrs. McMillan: ". . .there was a negro murderer in the jail, who had killed his wife; slashed her throat with a razor so that, her whole head tossing further and further backward from the bloody regurgitation of her bubbling throat, she ran out the cabin door and for six or seven steps up the quiet moonlit lane."

Southern newspapers of that period published full-length stories about the lynching of Nelse Patton. *The Lafayette County Press,* of September 9, 1908, printed the most complete and accurate account. This story, reprinted below, shows how Southern reporters wrote about such crimes in those old days. This is a colorful (perhaps too much so) and factual version of a story that was of great interest to William Faulkner. The mistakes are in the original.

NEGRO BRUTE CUTS WOMAN'S THROAT

Mrs. Mattie McMullen, A White Woman The Victim—Lived But Ten Minutes After The Tragedy. Sheriff Hartsfield And Posse of Citizens Give Chase and Land Negro in Jail

---

Mob Storms Jail and Kills Desperado

Officers and Guards Overpowered, and Failing to Find the Keys the Orderly Mob Quietly and Deliberately Took Matters in Their Own Hands, Forced Entrance to Cell Where Negro Was Confined Negro Armed with Poker Puts Up Desperate Fight and is Killed.

One of the coldest blooded murders and most brutal crimes known to the criminal calendar was perputrated one mile north of town yesterday morning about ten oclock, when a black brute of unsavory reputation by the name of Nelse Patton attacked Mrs. Mattie McMullen,[1] a respected white woman, with a razor, cutting her throat from ear to ear and causing almost instant death. Reports as to the cause of the tragedy vary, but as near as can be learned the partic- are these:

Mrs. McMullen, whose husband was confined at the time in the county jail at this place, was a hard working woman living alone with her 17-year-old daughter and two other very small children. It seems that Mr. Mc-Mullen wanted to communicate with his wife, and as was his custom as such occasions, he called the murderer, who was a "trusty" prisoner at the jail, to carry the missive. Arriving at the house, the negro, who was in an intoxicated condition, walked into the house without knocking and took a seat. Seeing the woman apparently alone and without protection, his animal passion was aroused and he made insulting remarks to her. He was ordered from the house and some angry words passed between them, when the woman started toward the bureau drawer to get her pistol, The brute seeing her design made a rush at the woman from behind and drawing the razor cut her throat from ear to ear, almost severing the head from the body. The dying woman rushed out of the house, and the daughter hearing the confusion rushed in, and was instantly grabbed by the negro. Jerking herself from the brutes grasp, she followed her mother who had fallen dead a few yards from the house. The daughter's screams alarmed the neighbors who quickly responded to call and immediately sent in a hurried telephone message to the Press office to summons officers and a physician, who in

1. The name was spelled in various ways by the newspapers of the time, and it is also pronounced several ways. As nearly as I can determine, it is McMillan.

less than twenty minutes were on the way to the scene of
the murder. The news spread like wild fire and it was
but a short while until the sheriff was joined by a posse
of citizens all in hot and close pursuit of the brute. After
chasing the negro three or four miles over fences, through
briars and fields he suddenly ran amuck of Johnny Cullen,
the 14-year-old son of Lin Cullen, who was out with
a double-barreled shotgun. Seeing the negro coming
towards him, he called a halt, but the negro paid no attention to the command and the boy let him have a load
of No. 5 shot in the chest, which slackened his speed
but did not stop him. The boy gave him another charge
in the left arm and side which stopped him. The negro
was at once surrounded by his pursuers and gladly gave
up. Over a hundred shots were fired from all kinds of
weapons but the negro was out of range. Being weak from
loss of blood, the brute was put on a horse and hurried to
jail.

As soon as the news spread of the capture, hundreds of
people began to gather around the jail and in small groups
about the street. They were not indulging in idle threats,
but from the seriousness of their expression one could see
the negro's fate was sealed.

Between nine and ten o'clock the crowd began swell-
ing to large proportions about the jail. Speeches were
made advocating letting the law take its course and vice-
versa, but patience had fallen far short of being a virtue
in a crowd like that. One wild shout went up, with a
rush the crowd advanced on the jail, pushing open doors
and jumping through windows. Officers and guards were
overpowered and disarmed. The keys could not be
found, but the hardware stores and blacksmith shops were
made to furnish the necessary tools and a set of quiet
and determined men plied them. Four and one-half
hours of hard and persistent work it took to break through
the thick walls of steel and masonry. The hall was at last
reached, and a search of the cell occupied by that black

fiend incarnate was made. It was at last found and broken into. Crouched and cringing in a dark corner of the cell, with the gleam of murder in his eye stood the miserable wretch armed with an iron poker awaiting the advance. In one, two, thee order the mob entered the cell, and in the same order the iron decended upon their heads, blood flew, the negro having all the advantage in his dark corner, held the crowd at bay and refused to come out. Only one thing was left to do. It was done. 26 pistol shots vibrated throughout the corridors of the solid old jail, and when the smoke cleared away the limp and lifeless body of the brute told the story.

The body was hustled down stairs to terra-firma, the rope was produced, the hangmans noose properly adjusted about the neck, and the drag to the court house yard began.

This morning the passerby saw the lifeless body of a negro suspended from a tree—it told the tale, that the murder of a white woman had been avenged—the public had done their duty. Following is the verdict of the Corners Jury:

We the Coroners Jury of inquest impaneled and sworn to investigate the death of Nelse Patton, colored find after inspecting the body and examining necessary witnesses that to the best of our knowledge and belief, the said Nelse Patton came to his death from gunshot or pistol wounds inflicted by parties to us unknown. That any one of a number of wounds would have been sufficient to cause death. We find further that Sheriff J. C. Hartsfield and his deputies were dilligent in their efforts to protect said Nelse Patton from the time of his arrest until they were overpowered by a mob of several hundred men who stormed the jail and dug their way through the walls until they reached the cell in which said Nelse Patton was confined and that said officers never surrendered the keys of jail or cells but that the locks were forced by some party or parties to us unknown and that the said Nelse Patton was shot with pistols or guns while in his cell and while attempting to protect himself with an iron rod. We further find that the said Nelse Patton was dead berore being brought from the jail and being hung.

Respectfully submitted,
E. O. Davidson
R. S. Adams
P. E. Matthews
B. P. Gray
A. F. Calloway
F. Wood

The papers gave special attention to Senator Sullivan's role in the lynching. This is a quotation from the Jackson *Daily Clarion-Ledger,* of Thursday morning, September 10, 1908. Errors are again reproduced from the original.

SULLIVAN'S HOT TALK ON OXFORD LYNCHING

FORMER UNITED STATES SENATOR FROM MISSISSIPPI LED THE MOB

(Associated Press Report)

Memphis, Tenn., Sept. 9.—A special from Oxford, Miss., quotes former U. S. Senator W. V. Sullivan as follows, with reference to the lynching of last night:

"I led the mob which lynched Nelse Patton and I am proud of it.

"I directed every movement of the mob, and I did everything I could to see that he was lynched.

"Cut a white woman's throat? and a negro? Of course I wanted him lynched.

"I saw his body dangling from a tree this morning and I am glad of it.

"When I heard of the horrible crime, I started to work immediately to get a mob. I did all I could to raise one. I was at the jail last night and I heard Judge Roane advise against lynching. I got up immediately after and urged the mob to lynch Patton.

"I aroused the mob and directed them to storm the jail.

"I had my revolver, but did not use it. I gave it to a deputy sheriff and told him: 'Shoot Patton and shoot to kill.'

"He used the revolver and shot. I suppose the bullets from my gun were some of those that killed the negro.

"I don't care what investigation is made, or what are the consequences. I am willing to stand them.

"I wouldn't mind standing the consequences any time for lynching a man who cut a white woman's throat. I will lead a mob in such a case any time."

XIV

The Snopeses

LAFAYETTE COUNTY citizens who have read Faulkner's books and those who have heard others tell stories about his notorious Snopeses can find a Snopes in almost every family and every business in the area. Every community, of course, has persons of the Snopes kind. The hunt for the real Snopeses has become like the parlor game of "Button, Button, Who's Got the Button?" But in Oxford's game of "Snopeses, Snopeses, Who Are the Snopeses?" everyone guesses, and everyone has a button and hopes that no one else will know it.

All the stories about the Snopeses are great exaggerations of actual persons and events. If a person as evil and devious as Flem Snopes had actually lived here, he would have been run out of the county or hanged on a blackjack oak after two or three of his tricks. People in Mississippi would not tolerate such a barnburner. Of course there are dishonest and cruel people here as in every community. But Faulkner has taken every crime and all the cheating and every instance of brutality he has remembered and told them all in his stories and novels, and time after time he has attributed these crimes and inhumanities to the Snopeses. As a whole, the Snopes stories result from

Faulkner's imaginative and inventive use of stories from life. He has pieced together and expanded all the worst traits of the worst people he has known. But one of my neighbors asked me what was unusual and interesting about our best people. I could give no answer.

Frenchman's Bend, I think, was Dutch Bend, and the Old Frenchman's Place may have been based on the old Prince* Place in that community. The Princes were Unionists during the Civil War, and in the days of Reconstruction they received a large sum of money from the government because Union soldiers had burned their cotton. Lem Prince* became the richest man in the county. The Princes moved from Dutch Bend to Tula and then into Oxford, and Lem started a bank—like Flem Snopes. In Dutch Bend also lived a man named Flem McCain, and Faulkner could have used his first name for the head of the Snopes clan, though I don't believe Flem McCain resembled Flem Snopes in many other ways. Bus Cook* was born in Dutch Bend, and he too moved to Tula and then to Oxford. Flem McCain and Bus Cook made a trip to Texas just as Flem Snopes did, and I believe they did bring some spotted ponies back and auction them off. Then they established a wholesale business in Oxford.

One episode in the life of Bus Cook was rather carefully followed in Faulkner's description of the career of Flem Snopes. Twice, once in the short story "Centaur in Brass" and once in *The Town*, Faulkner has told a story about Flem Snopes stealing brass from the power plant in Jefferson. More than fifty years ago here in Oxford, Bus Cook was accused of stealing brass. A plump little man who always wore a white

shirt and a black bow tie, Bus was superintendent of the water works and the light plant at that time.
He did not seem to have even the slightest qualification
for this job, and no one knew why he was ever made
superintendent. The sexual prowess of Mrs. Cook was
not his qualification as Eula Varner Snopes's was for
Flem.

Joe Butler, a tall, keen, black-eyed natural mechanic, was night engineer. Joe's father died when
Joe was only a boy, leaving him an invalid mother
and three little sisters to take care of. Times were
hard then, but by hard work Joe managed to provide
for them. Two of his sisters married, had children,
then lost their husbands through death, and returned
home destitute—adding to the burden Joe was already
carrying. Yet he always remained cheerful, never
complained, and carried on until all of them were old
enough to provide for themselves. By this time Joe
was nearly fifty years old. Such men are rare, and they
are of little interest to the public, because they are
never connected with any big crime or scandal.

Old Major Peguese had been firing the old steam
boilers since before I can remember. He was a big,
heavy, flat-nosed Negro, who was probably five feet,
ten inches tall and weighed about 250 pounds. He
was always good-natured and ready to smile, showing
a big mouth full of pearly white teeth and two big,
gold-crowned front ones. Major was prompt, reliable,
and honest. As long as the steam boilers were used,
he fired for the city of Oxford, and I believe
that he retired on a pension from the town
after the change to diesels. He and his family
lived well as long as he lived. They traded at
the store of a good friend of mine, who remarked to

me that he was always glad to sell them anything they wanted on credit. I did not know Major's wife, but I think she was much younger than he was. Old Major is gone now, but his wife and children are still living in the home that Major owned in Freedman Town.

George Rivers, the other Negro fireman, was a wiry little man, and he too was liked by everyone. We called him Scrap. He lived on a small farm about two miles from Oxford and drove a buggy to his work each day. From the time when I was a little boy, I knew Uncle George and his wife, whom we white children called Aunt Bell. They never had trouble with anyone. While Scrap fired at the power plant, Aunt Bell worked their orchard and truck patches. She was an extraordinary cook, a hard worker, and very thrifty. How she could can so much fruit and put up so much good food was always a mystery to me. Many times when we boys were passing along the road in front of their home, she would bawl us out for not stopping, make us come in, and give us a big piece of fine cake and a dish of fruit. On the other hand, we always shared the game we killed and the fish we caught with Aunt Bell and Uncle George. They always did more for us than we could do for them. They had many friends. While I was in the army during World War I, a storm destroyed their old home. When I came back, they were living in a better home than they had ever owned before. Aunt Bell told me that by subscription the people, mostly white friends, had raised the money to pay for their home. Both Uncle George and Aunt Bell are gone. Their house still stands. A white man now lives in it.

I heard my father say that Mr. Bus Cook was leaving his job as superintendent of our water and light plant because he was accused of selling a lot of old water meters and scrap brass and pocketing the money. It was not proved that he was guilty, and if anything was done about it, I never heard about it. My guess is that Faulkner got from Joe Butler the idea of having Flem steal the pop-off valves and gauges. Joe's sarcasm and contempt would probably have caused him to remark, after someone had stolen brass, that he expected the valves and gauges to be next.

In *The Town* the Negro firemen Tom Tom and Tomey's Turl put all the stolen brass in the town water tank. Oxford's water tank still stands just as it did when Bus Cook stole the brass. It is at least 150 feet from the ground. If it had been filled with gold and if Uncle George and Major had been told that they could have all they would climb up there and get, all that gold would still be up there. They would have been afraid to climb it. The brass in the water tank is pure invention.

These were the people that Faulkner wrote his story about. Perhaps this story tells more about Faulkner's writing than it would have if it had been proved that brass actually was in the water tank. Faulkner did not need a great deal to base his fiction on. The yarn about the big Negro putting on a gown and arming himself with a butcher knife in order to catch the little Negro who had cuckolded him is not based on these characters. It is probably derived from a story told about Lucius Coleman, a Negro who has been the basis for some of the fabrications told in our hunting camps. Faulkner gave Scrap his character, and Lucius fits some of the description. He tells some very tall tales.

Jim Packs* was another source for Faulkner's Flem Snopes. After Faulkner's grandfather had to resign, Jim became president of the First National Bank. Shrewd and unscrupulous, Jim did not mind betraying a man's confidence and using what information he had learned to his own advantage. When a man needed to borrow money, Jim first gave him a lecture on farming with mules. And then he would ask what the man planned to do with the money he borrowed. If it was a good deal, Jim would send somebody else out and make the profit himself—just as Flem Snopes buys the goats before Ratliff can in *The Hamlet*. Some Yankees bought a farm next to Jim Packs's place in Cypress Creek Bottom. They had great faith in the honesty of the Negroes, and they planned to show the people around here how to farm. Mr. Packs was bootlegging to the Negroes, and they would pick the Yankees' cotton and take about half of it to Mr. Packs and trade it to him for whisky and money. He got rich off these Yankee owners before they discovered what was happening to their cotton.

Perhaps Faulkner took the story about Ike Snopes's sodomy with the cow from an actual episode. A Negro who worked for John Falkner's mother-in-law was caught having sexual intercourse with a cow. Like I. O. Snopes in *The Town* and the short story "Mule in the Yard," one man who lived here nearly fifty years ago drove his old pore mules on the railroad track to get them killed and to collect money from the railroad.

The most important event in the life of Mink Snopes—the murder of Jack Houston in *The Hamlet*—was based on a well-known crime that happened in Lafayette County in 1910. When I was a child, my father, Linburn Cullen, owned an old ten-gauge, breech-loading, lever-action shotgun. All the four boys in our family did our first hunting with that old gun. Mr. Pete Callicoat borrowed the gun, and just before the quail season opened, I walked down to his house about four miles south of Oxford to get the gun. When I arrived, he was not at home. His wife, whom we called Miss Gena, let me have the gun, but remarked that she was sorry that I had come for it. Walking the road back to Oxford, I met Mr. Taylor* and his son, who were both riding horseback. They asked me if I had met Mr. Callicoat, and I told them that I had not. They rode on.

Shortly after this, I met Mr. Callicoat, who was riding a horse, and he asked me if I had met the Taylors and wanted to know if they had asked me any questions. I said that they had asked if I had met him. Then he asked what I had told them.

I told them, I said, that I had not met him. He was sorry about this, because he expected the Taylors to waylay him and kill him on the road to his home.

The Taylors lived on an adjoining farm owned by Mr. Marvin Stovall*. Pete Callicoat claimed that they were the tools of Mr. Stovall and that they had been trying to run him out of the neighborhood so that Mr. Stovall would be able to buy the Callicoat farm cheap. The Taylors had taken an old, worn-out horse down into his cornfield and shot it to death. Then they had made out a warrant for his arrest and charged him with killing the horse. Pete said that their charge was a frame-up and that my father, knowing that I was coming for the shotgun, had loaned him his old forty-five Colt pistol. In town, Pete had met the Taylors, and he would have killed them if someone had not knocked his pistol up when he tried to shoot them. The Taylors had run and got away. Now he expected them to shoot him in the back. He planned to turn off the main road and ride his horse to his home on an abandoned old road. He got home without trouble that afternoon, but the Taylors must have guessed what he had done.

The next morning when he started back to town by the same route, he was shot in the back of his head with buckshot. Taylor, as the evidence proved, had been hiding in a ditch and had waited there for some time before Pete came by. The court records say that Taylor shot Callicoat "by the side of a small open thicket, in the corn field and while in some thirty or forty feet of the road." After Mr. Callicoat fell from his horse, Taylor went to him, pulled his pistol from its holster, fired it, then took a forty-five bullet and hammered it into his gun stock. This was also proved by the hammer marks on the stock. Late that afternoon Taylor came to Oxford and reported that he had met Callicoat, who had shot at him. His gun stock, Taylor claimed, had caused the bullet to glance off and miss him. Then he had shot Callicoat in self-defense. No one believed him. At his trial for murder he pleaded guilty and saved his neck. He was sentenced to life in the state penitentiary. It was never proved that Mr. Stovall had any connection with the murder.

All the facts in this case lead me to believe that this is the crime which William Faulkner used as a basis for his story in *The Hamlet* about Mink Snopes's murdering Jack Houston. The main similarities are the quarrel about a farm animal, the ten-gauge shotgun, the ambush and shooting in the back, and the place where it happened. Faulkner describes it as "the thicket where he crouched and the dim faint road which ran beside it."

No one is interested in good and loyal citizens because they are usual. Even I can't be interested in them unless I catch them doing some ridiculous stunt. But we do have 9999½ good citizens for every one Taylor or Snopes. Outsiders read Faulkner's books and think the people of our county are all ignorant heathen. Not all of us are.

It is hard for me to believe that the shy and almost prudish William Faulkner I have known could have written *The Hamlet*. This story of low-class people living in Mississippi is greatly exaggerated. After reading the stories about the Snopeses, I wish that William had written more about some of the noble people here in our county whom I knew.

XV

The Town

THE MINOR CHARACTERS and the short episodes William Faulkner describes in *The Town* are probably more carefully derived from real persons and events than those in any other work of his that I have read. A number of details in the novel suggest that Faulkner has given background to the novel by making it almost a miscellany of anecdotes that have been told about Oxford.

William remembers well the time when we escorted his honor, the mayor of Oxford, out of town on a rail and decorated him with tar and chicken feathers. Mayor De Spain of Jefferson has to leave town after the suicide of his mistress, Eula Varner Snopes. If Faulkner had in mind the real story about a mayor leaving Oxford, he certainly did change things around. Mayor Adams in *The Town* has the same name as the real Mayor Adams who was tarred and feathered.

For a long time this hypocritical old sot had pretended to be a great crusader for law and decency by giving everyone brought before him a vitriolic lecture on evil ways. He had levied heavy fines on the boys. But he drank all the bootleg whisky which he confiscated from them. One night during a friendly poker game in a livery stable, the boys ran out of refreshments, and a runner went to acquire some more. On this errand he saw his honor going into the cabin of a high-brown Negro woman. When he came back, the poker game broke up, and its members converged around the cabin, pushed the door open, and captured his honor in his long-johns as he leaped from the bed of the Negro woman. The boys had his honor right where they wanted him, and they were not forgetting his tongue-lashings about drinking a little whisky. He begged and pleaded to ears that ignored his pleas for mercy, and he even begged on the grounds of his family—but to no avail. He was escorted to the outskirts of Oxford, given a few dabs of warm tar and chicken feathers, and told to keep going. He was a sight to remember, dressed in his long-johns with his big bloated body and small legs decorated with tar and chicken feathers. He reminded me of a huge toad frog as he disappeared into the night.

About fifty years ago a young natural mechanic, John Buffaloe, lived in Oxford. After long months of work in his spare time, he announced that he had built a horseless carriage and that he would demonstrate it on the square on the following Saturday afternoon. For the next week the coming show of a horseless carriage was the talk all over the county.

People for miles around Oxford drove buggies and wagons to town and brought their families to see the show. They hitched their teams to a log chain that ran through holes in posts and encircled the courthouse with the exception of the four walkways. After buying their supplies and placing them in their vehicles, they gathered in the courthouse yard to greet old friends and neighbors, discuss the weather and the crops, and pass on the gossip from their neighborhoods.

When the time came for John to demonstrate, we crowded along the fence around the courthouse yard, feeling pretty sure we were safe even if John's horseless carriage did get out of control. Then John cranked up. Mufflers hadn't been invented in those days. As he drove around the square with his motor wide open and backfiring about every fifth stroke, it sounded like a war. The poor horses and mules hitched to the log chain had never seen such a noisy, dangerous-sounding critter before. They went wild with fear, broke loose their halters, squealed, kicked, and ran wildly out of town, scattering groceries, wagon wheels, and buggy parts on trees and gateposts for miles around town, leaving their owners and all their families to walk home from town, in some cases several miles.

Poor John, his dream of starting a horseless carriage business turned to ashes. People said that they were impractical and dangerous and that such hair-brained young fellows should be brought under control before they tore up the world. Our indignant city fathers met that night in special meeting and passed an ordinance levying a fine on anyone who drove a car within a mile of the courthouse. I am told that this ordinance was repealed just a few years ago.

I am sure that William Faulkner saw this show. He tells this same story in *The Town*, though he changes John Buffaloe's name to Joe Buffaloe: "The city electrician (the one who kept the town's generators and dynamos and transformers working) was a genius. One afternoon in 1904 he drove out of his back yard into the street in the first automobile we had ever seen, made by hand completely, engine and all, from magneto coil to radius rod, and drove into the Square at the moment when Colonel Sartoris the banker's surrey and blooded matched team were crossing it on the way home. Although Colonel Sartoris and his driver were not hurt and the horses when caught had no scratch on them and the electrician offered to repair the surrey (it was said he even offered to put a gasoline engine in it this time), Colonel Sartoris appeared in person before the next meeting of the board of aldermen, who passed an edict that no gasoline-propelled vehicle should ever operate on the streets of Jefferson."

The short story "Uncle Willie," parts of which Faulkner used in *The Town,* is so true that I can remember the actual basis of almost all of it, except for the death of Uncle Willie. When Uncle Bob Chilton, who provided the basis for this character, died, I was away from Oxford, and I do not know how he died.

Chilton's drug store is one of the first places of business in Oxford that I can remember. Two brothers, Mr. Top and Mr. Bob Chilton, sold drugs, ran a soda fountain, and also sold such miscellaneous things as marbles, baseball equipment, and slingshot rubbers. The drug store was noted for its fine ice cream made from rich Jersey cow milk and eggs by old Ad Bush, the Chiltons' ex-slave houseboy and cook. Ad was the Negro who cooked for us for many years on our camping trips in the Delta. He was one of the finest chefs and cooks I have ever known. I do not believe that I have ever eaten ice cream as good as that sold by the Chiltons. Naturally the drug store was a great gathering place for the young people of Oxford.

Mr. Top, a fat, bald-headed man with wide shoulders, was full of fun and jokes. When kids would go into the store to buy a top, he would spin around and say "Here it is," then laugh, and sell us a top. Mr.

Top lived on what was then called South Street in the same block as the Falkners, the Kings, the Old-hams, and the Logans. Mr. Bob lived at the end of a street at the edge of town. He kept about ten fine Jersey cows to furnish the milk for ice cream served at the fountain, and he had a faithful, trustworthy old Negro by the name of Abe Wiley, who kept house for him, kept up the yard, and fed and milked the cows. Our land joined Mr. Bob's well-kept thirty acres. Carefree as I was then, I had great admiration and respect for Mr. Bob and his fine management. He turned his milk into ice cream and sold it for three dollars per gallon while others were glad to get twenty cents per gallon. One remark that he made to me I will never forget. He said that if he had the strength to work as I did he would become a millionaire, and I believe he would have.

While in the prime of life, Mr. Top suddenly died, leaving Mr. Bob to run the business alone for many years. He continued to live as an old bachelor with old Abe keeping house for him. By attending strictly to business and managing well, he amassed a small fortune. Never did I know him to have anything to do with women or seem to take the slightest interest in them. Never had I known him to dissipate in any way.

At about this time I left Oxford for several years. When I returned home, Mr. Bob was still quietly running the drug store, old Abe was still milking his cows, and old Ad was still making ice cream for him. Chilton's drug store was still the popular hang-out for the young folks of Oxford. At about this time Mr. Bob, who had never owned a car, bought one. The town gossips circulated the report that he was drinking heavily. He began making trips to Memphis with his Negro chauffeur. At this time he was in his sixties. How he did it I do not know, but he began having dates with some of the best-looking young ladies in Oxford; among them was one of my old flames. She was a good-looking high-stepper, but I think she should have had a price tag pinned on her.

What happened to Mr. Bob I will never know. Maybe he heard the call of the wild and was trying to make up for lost time. Spending money did not mean anything to him any more. Because he had traded his life and youth for money, perhaps he changed to hate money, realized his mistake, and crowded all the living and fun he could into the short time he had to live. At any rate, he was going strong—out with a new young woman nearly every time anyone saw him in Memphis. He really was a good-time papa to the pretty gold-diggers up in Memphis when I saw him last. Mr. Bob and Uncle Willie were alike in owning a drug store, in being close to young boys, and in having a thrilling last fling in their old age.

Matt Levitt's courtship of Linda Snopes and his fight with some of the local boys is based on a story about a boxer named Chamberlin who came to Oxford and whipped four or five Oxford boys after an argument about a girl. The blacksmith Uncle Noon Gatewood in *The Town* is a fairly accurate portrait of the old Negro blacksmith Gilbert Isom. One paragraph in *The Town* is an especially good example of how accurately and carefully Faulkner sometimes bases his fiction on life in Oxford: ". . . ours was a town founded by Aryan Baptists and Methodists, for Aryan Baptists and Methodists. We had a Chinese laundryman and two Jews, brothers with their families, who ran two clothing stores. But one of them had been trained in Russia to be a rabbi and spoke seven languages including classic Greek and Latin and worked geometry problems for relaxation and he was absolved, lumped in the same absolution with old Doctor Wyott, president emeritus of the Academy (his grandfather had founded it), who could read not only Greek and Hebrew but Sanskrit too, who wore two foreign decorations for (we, Jefferson, believed) having been not just a professing but a militant and even boasting atheist for at least sixty of his eighty years. . .; and the other Jewish brother and his family and the Chinese all attended, were members of, the Methodist church and so they didn't count either, being in our eyes merely non-white people, not actually colored. And although the Chinese was definitely a colored man even if not a Negro, he was only he, single peculiar and barren; not just kinless but even kindless, half the world or anyway half the continent (we all knew about San Francisco's Chinatown) sundered from his like and therefore as threatless as a mule."

The two Jews who lived in Oxford and ran two clothing stores were Joe and Heinman Friedman. They came from Russia, and Heinman was trained to be a rabbi. One of the Jewish families often attended the Methodist church. Old Dr. Wyatt was president emeritus of the military academy in Oxford. The Chinese laundryman, Hum Wo, ran a laundry on Depot Street. For a long time he was a solitary figure, but in his last years he associated with the colored people. He lived with a Negro woman, but they had no children. So in that respect he was, I suppose, "as threatless as a mule."

Except for names, Faulkner has used local events and people with such careful detail in his stories that things I had long forgotten return to my memory as I read his fiction.

XVI

The Mansion

READING FAULKNER'S *The Mansion* made me see many old friends of long ago and remember many things which I had forgotten about the past. Even the picture on the cover reminded me of the old home of Faulkner's grandfather. It faced South Lamar Street, but years ago it was cut up into apartments and turned around to front University Avenue. With an uncanny memory and almost perfect accuracy Faulkner has described the old Oxford: the town, the courthouse, the depot and railroad, the trains, the horse-drawn hacks, and the people of Oxford at that time.

At train time crowds of men and boys and dogs gathered at the old depot to see who came in on the trains. The train whistled for Stone's Crossing one half mile from the depot. As it glided into the station, the fireman rang the bell, and the crowds smelled the coal smoke of the engine.

The Negro porters jumped off, placed little boxes for steps, and helped the passengers off the train. Negro boys from the old Commercial and Colonial hotels yelled, "Commercial Hotel, Mister," or "Colonial Hotel, Mister. Take your grip, Mister." Fine ladies and drummers got off the train, followed by farmers and townspeople. And last of all a bunch of

our country youths tumbled out of the train, return-
ing home from seeing the sights up in Memphis.
Some of them could not remember all they had seen.
Several horse-drawn hacks waited to haul the passengers the half mile up the hill to the town square. The
streets were not paved, and the sidewalks were made
of plank. It was not stylish to walk, and since it cost
only a quarter to ride a hack anywhere in town, most
folks rode.

Oxford is a little town, and everybody knows gossip and scandals that are whispered across backyard
fences, and no one can ever be sure of how much truth
is in them. But I never heard of many of the incidents Faulkner uses in his fiction. Most of his characters are inventions. By using a real background and
knowing the cussedness to be found in humanity everywhere, Faulkner creates stories which remind me of
events and people that Faulkner might not have had
in mind when he was writing the story.

Many people tell a story about a young woman who
would have given birth to a bastard if her father had
not hired a prideless no-account to marry her. That
young man, however, never became president of a
bank as Flem Snopes did. Faulkner probably heard
the same story, and it may be the basis of his story
about Eula Varner, but probably he had no particular
person actually in mind as he wrote. I went to school
with a girl who resembled Eula, but I considered her
a good girl. No exact model for Eula lived in Lafayette County or anywhere else, but affairs like Eula's
happen everywhere.

I remember very well the last bear hunt in Lafayette County, and the complete story may show how
Faulkner selects some details and omits others. That's

what makes it hard to give the full background for
even one of the little casual incidents in his stories.
Whenever Faulkner writes about actual events that
he remembers, he uses the details that are most suitable
to the character he is writing about. In *The Mansion* Mink Snopes remembers the last bear hunt in
Yoknapatawpha County: ". . .two, three years ago it
was when Solon Quick or Vernon Tull or whoever it
was had seen the bear, the last bear in that part of
the county, when it ran across Varner's mill dam
and into the thicket, and . . . the hunt had been
organised and somebody rode a horse in to Jefferson
to get hold of Ike McCaslin and Walter Ewell, the
best hunters in the county, and they came out with
their buckshot big-game shells and the bear and deer
hounds and set the standers and drove the bottom
where the bear had been seen but it was gone by
then."

One morning in the early fall Walter Miller (Uncle
Bud), who is like Faulkner's Walter Ewell in some
ways, came to me and told me that a Negro farm hand
had ridden down to a spring to water his mule and
that a big bear which had been drinking from the
spring rose up on its hind feet to greet him. This
Negro reported that because he had more confidence
in his own speed than in the mule's he had left the
mule to take care of itself. Uncle Bud, Bob Harkins,
and I went to see if this story was true. It was. The
ground was very wet from recent heavy rains, and it
was easy to follow the tracks of the big bear.

The bear was first seen about twenty miles from
Oxford, near what is known as Malone's Tank, a
watering tank on the I. C. railroad in Marshall County. That day we tracked the bear down Spring Creek

Bottom into Tallahatchie Bottom about fifteen miles from Oxford. By dusk the next day we had tracked him to where he crossed Highway 30 about three miles east of Oxford. As we gathered in Oxford the next morning, Captain Jack Hume reported seeing his tracks crossing the road near Bell Rivers' home, about three miles southeast of Oxford. Because Bob was the best tracker, we let him follow the bear's trail, and Uncle Bud and I tried to head him off before he got into Yocona Bottom. If I had stayed at home, I could have shot the bear from my front porch. My sister-in-law saw him cross our yard; she rushed to a telephone and told the people up-town that the bear had just passed through the yard. As I drove up the road I saw a great crowd of men and boys armed with shotguns, rifles, pistols, axes, and pitchforks cross the road in front of me. We had no bear dogs, but Gurvis McCain said he would put his coon dogs on the trail as soon as we could find fresh tracks. When he saw the bear's tracks, he backed out. I got ahead of the crowd and saw where the bear had gone into a swamp thicket. Because the crowd was following him, I went around to the other side of the thicket. But the crowd did not follow him into the swamp and he stayed in there. After waiting some time, I returned to his trail, followed him into the thicket, and ran him out by the crowd. As Bob Harkins raised his gun to shoot, a little Negro boy saw the bear and ran between Bob and the bear hollering, "Here 'e go! Here 'e go!"

The boy prevented Bob from shooting, and the bear ran out of sight. Bob did not often cuss, but that time he did. As he lowered his gun, he said, "The only damn nigger in the county who ever chased a bear, and he did it at the wrong time."

Then Ed Newman came up with some hounds, and they went over the hill at high speed barking "Yo! Yo!" at every breath. Soon I met the hounds coming back with their tails tucked between their legs. They never realized what they were after until they saw the bear. We were all fagged out, and to make it worse, we got a message saying that this was an old bear used by the late Paul Rainey to train his dogs and that if we killed it we would be prosecuted to the full extent of the law. After Rainey's death the bear had been released. We had believed that this bear had been driven to the hills by the high water over the Mississippi River bottom. All of us were fed up on bear hunting for quite a while.

Elsewhere in *The Mansion,* Charles Mallison tells a story about some people that I knew well. "There was Tug Nightingale. His father was the cobbler, with a little cubbyhole of a shop around a corner off the Square—a little scrawny man who wouldn't have weighed a hundred pounds with his last and bench and all his tools in his lap, with a fierce moustache which hid most of his chin too, and fierce undefeated intolerant eyes—a Hard-Shell Baptist who didn't merely have to believe it, because he knew it was so: that the earth was flat and that Lee had betrayed the whole South when he surrendered at Appomattox. He was a widower. Tug was his only surviving child. Tug had got almost as far as the fourth grade when the principal himself told Mr. Nightingale it would be better for Tug to quit."

Most of my life I knew of Mr. Peacock, who ran a shoe repair shop for many years in a little cubbyhole located at the second door on the east side of South Lamar Street. Faulkner's description of Tug's father fits Mr. Peacock exactly, but the statements that he was in the Civil War and that he said that "General Lee had been a coward and a traitor" are, I feel sure, only fiction. But if that was what Mr. Peacock thought, that is just what he would have said. He was outspoken.

Mr. Peacock lived until he was ninety-six years old. Once when he was more than ninety years old, he and I had just come out of the Green Fern, which was run by Miss Dorothy Oldham, Faulkner's sister-in-law. We had drunk a few beers and talked of old times and old friends. The sidewalks were crowded, and we met two big, rude young men who were roughly pushing everyone out of their way and taking all the sidewalk. I wondered if they would have the decency to respect that old man. When I saw that they did not, I clouted the one in front a good lick on his jaw and knocked them both off the sidewalk into the street. As they stood there looking at us, not a word was spoken. The biggest one rubbed his jaw, then quietly walked around us and on down the street. I looked around. There stood Mr. Peacock with his walking stick held high above his head, ready to take part in the fight. He said that he was not going to let two of them attack me.

Faulkner gave Joe the name Tug. I first met him in the fall, just after school opened. He was a new boy in school, and he looked too cocky to suit me. As we met in the hall of the old Oxford Grammar School, I gave him a good hard punch on the shoulder to introduce myself to him and see how he would like it. Joe's face turned red; he sputtered, turned around, spit out a mouthful of tobacco, and walloped me in the belly as hard as he could. I returned the wallop, and then we stood toe to toe, both slugging each other. Each time I hit him I almost prayed for him to say enough, but the little runt was as tough as a pine knot. I was very happy when the teacher broke it up in time to save me from having to say uncle. Neither of us ever forgot that introduction. Each of us always said that the other won that fight, and neither of us ever wanted to try it over.

Before moving to Oxford, Joe had gone to school very little. Where he had lived out in the hills there were few schools, and these were far apart. Like his father before him, he could not remember when he began chewing tobacco and drinking whisky. About this time I heard a story about Joe's country-school days. I do not know it to be true, but it fits Joe like a glove. Several of the boys were known to be drinking whisky and using tobacco. One morning the teacher brought a bottle of whisky, some tobacco juice, live worms, and glasses. She planned to demonstrate the harmful effects of tobacco and whisky. After showing that the worms were alive and wiggling, she dropped them into the glasses. Then she poured a little whisky over the worms in one glass and the tobacco juice over the worms in the other glass. After a few furious wiggles, the worms in both glasses were dead. She then asked the pupils if this demonstration had taught them anything. Joe raised his hand and told her that it had "larnt" him that if you would drink plenty of whisky and chew plenty of tobacco you would never be wormy.

Just as Faulkner says, Joe quit school early. So far as I know, he never had anything to do with the horse and mule dealers like Faulkner's Pat Stamper. Like Tug Nightingale, Joe Peacock was a house painter. Both joined the army in 1917 and both went overseas as cooks. After the war Joe came home and resumed painting and paper-hanging. He lived frugally, saved his money, and supported his old mother and father for many years. His younger sister married and had three children. After a long illness with tuberculosis, her husband died. Joe then supported her and educated her children. Faulkner made Tug only a poor fence-and-barn painter, but Joe was a fairly successful contractor. He could have written a check for ten thousand dollars at any time. He had a bad habit of carrying a thousand or two dollars on his person. I tried to get him not to do this because I was afraid someone would rob him, but no one ever did. Joe was tight with his money, but a friend could get anything he had. Once my home burned, and I lost all my belongings. Joe called me off to one side, pulled out that roll, and said, "John, do you need any money? If you do, you can have anything I've got." I did not take a cent. I figured we could get along without it. Old Joe Peacock was one of the finest friends I ever had.

While painting in the county courthouse, Joe fell from a high scaffold and broke several bones and shattered his knee. Joe never recovered from that fall. He began drinking more and more whisky to deaden the pains he suffered. After a short time, he had spent his savings of a lifetime of hard work. When I heard he was planning to sell his home, I told him that the men who were hanging around him and helping him drink up everything he had would turn on him when he went broke. Joe was pretty far gone then. He said that he did not give a damn. When he went broke he would never ask anyone for anything but would blow his damn brains out. A short time after that I passed him on the street. He was walking as though in a trance and did not even recognize me. He had a look on his face I will never forget. I stopped and watched as he walked away from me. I knew he was not responsible and something ought to be done for him. That night at home I still thought of him and decided that I would try to get him into a sanitarium the next day. That night he was jailed for drunkenness. He begged for some whisky and said he would die if he did not get a drink. His pleas were ignored. Next morning Joe was found dead in the cell. His heart had quit on him. In his pocket they found one lone five-dollar bill. I will always regret that we let this fine man die in a jail cell under the charge of drunkenness. He belonged in a hospital.

Faulkner seems to be describing Lee Baggette and Scotchy McCall when he describes Captain McLendon, the commander, and Scotchy, the first sergeant, of that company that they formed here at Oxford in 1917. Mrs. Baggette, Lee's mother, was a big, heavy woman. Lee himself was a ginner and cotton buyer and gambled on the stock market. I have often wondered how he got himself elected captain of that company.

Two Finns in *The Mansion* were liberal and possibly communist. Faulkner writes that "They simply took it for granted that there was a proletariat in Jefferson as specific and obvious and recognisable as the day's climate, and as soon as they learned English they would find it and, all being proletarians together, they would all be communists together too as was not only their right and duty but they couldn't help themselves." They were not Finns, but Swedes. They were both fine painters and interior decorators. Except for believing in socialism, they were honorable, hard-working, thrifty citizens. The little one, Gus Youth (Faulkner calls him "a little quick-tempered irreconcilable hornet"), still lives here; he married a girl that was raised across the garden from me. They have brought up a fine family. If everyone had principles as good as Gus Youth's, socialism might work. At any rate our country is doing more and more of the things he advocates every day. He made the people awful mad by going down to the Negro high school and making talks, as Linda Snopes does in *The Mansion*. So the FBI was notified. They investigated and nothing was done. I also know the Negro principal of the high school and would expect him to make remarks about like the ones he says in *The Mansion*: " 'Then you know yourself it wont work. That you are not ready for it yet and neither are we. . . . That we have got to make the white people need us first. . . . So we have got to make a place of our own in your culture and economy too. . . . Let us have your friendship all the time, and your help when we need it. But keep your patronage until we ask for it.' " I consider him a good citizen. Faulkner calls him "the intelligent dedicated man with his composed and tragic face." He is working for the advancement of his color in the only right way: trying to teach them to be clean, intelligent, courteous, useful citizens.

Jensen, the other immigrant, was a big hard-working man who never did learn to speak English well. Faulkner describes him as "puzzled and bewildered," "practically without human language, a troglodyte."

After he came to Oxford his wife came from Denmark, and they married here, I understand. Mr. Jensen is dead but Mrs. Jensen still lives at Memphis, Tennessee. They had one fine daughter who was very bright in school here. She is now married to a doctor in Memphis.

During the prohibition era just after World War I, many concoctions were brewed and sold to men who wanted liquor. Many men lost their lives and health drinking these concoctions. Many learned they could get high by drinking Jew Maker Ginger. Someone put a brand of this ginger on the market. It paralyzed and killed many of the people who drank it. It had an effect similar to polio, and it was common to see someone who was paralyzed with withered legs from its effect. People like this were called Jakelegs. From this I think William Faulkner invented the name of Jakeleg Watterman for his bootlegging character. It is a very appropriate name. Though Jakeleg Watterman is probably a fictitious name, as long as I can remember since dear old Mississippi supposedly went dry, we have had such places as Jakeleg's Camp, and we still have them. Why we allow the preachers and the bootleggers to dominate us is beyond me. For my part I am ashamed of it, but that is the way it is.

Faulkner's treatment of Mink Snopes in *The Mansion* proves again that he understands and in many ways admires what some people call the poor white. No group of people on earth has more of that kind of fierce independence than the poor backwoods, uneducated people of Mississippi. Mink's good qualities exist all over the South among the pure Anglo-Saxon stock who pioneered it and who have had little contact with the outside world. They will die for what they believe to be right, as they have proved many times on the battlefield. Alvin York, a hero in World War I, was one of this breed. There have been many others. Faulkner did a wonderful job in creating a person like Mink Snopes, especially in describing how Mink at the end felt that the ground was soaking up his life. A primitive person like Mink who was worn out with life would probably feel that he was being drawn back to the earth. Gravity would make him feel that way.

Many fine men and beautiful women who have the capacity to love and be loved destroy themselves. And like Gavin Stephens, I myself ask, "Why, oh why, did they do it?" Faulkner is no preacher and neither am I, yet his stories about living humanity remind me of the teachings of Ecclesiastes. No man can ever picture the life of mankind more truly. Human nature is the same today that it was at that time. I have watched the ways of men here in Oxford or Jefferson, as he calls it, and I know that his stories are truly based on humanity.

I hope we are at last rid of the Snopeses. They have been hard on our reputation here in Mississippi. There is nothing new under the sun. Man is just now finding out a lot of things he did not know until lately.

XVII

Faulkner's Own South

IN AN ISSUE of *Ford Times,* William Faulkner tells how he and Malcolm Cowley were traveling over a mountain in New England. They stopped and asked two farmers if the road went over the mountain. They said that it did. So Faulkner and Cowley started to drive away. After they had gone about fifty yards, Cowley suddenly stopped, backed up, and asked, "Can we get over the mountain?" The men said, "No, we don't believe you can." Faulkner contends that this is typical of New Englanders.

Things would be very different from that in Mississippi. "In my own South," Faulkner writes, "the two Mississippians would have adopted us before Cowley could have closed his mouth and put the car in motion again, saying, one of them, the other would already be getting into the car, 'Why, sure, it won't be no trouble at all. Jim here will go with you and I'll telephone across the mountain for my nephew to meet you with his truck where you are stuck. It'll pull you right on through and he'll even have a mechanic waiting with a new crankcase.' "

William may exaggerate here a little, but there is truth in the story. Mississippians and Southerners have, I believe, a collective personality at least in some ways, and in this anecdote as in all his works Faulkner has shown remarkable understanding of the Southerner and his ways.

Lafayette County provided history and manners and legends. From boyhood Faulkner listened, took note of the stories, and then wrote about them in his own way. He would have been a great writer regardless of his environment, but he did have some wonderful things to write about here in Lafayette County: beautiful hills and valleys and woods; wild life; a county with a unique history of its own; and characters of remarkable diversity and individuality.

Faulkner had contrasting classes of people to write about. The people that settled in Oxford, Mississippi, and Lafayette County were mostly descendants of early immigrants from England and Ireland and Scotland. They moved here, made their settlements, and cut their roads through the wilderness. They were a neighborly people because people had to be good neighbors in frontier days. And they still are. As years rolled by, classes became apparent, hill people and plantation owners. The hill people were just poor people who homesteaded or bought land for practically nothing. Sons and daughters would marry and move from one hollow over into another. They would build a log cabin and settle down to a primitive life, and the parents would give them a heifer calf and a wash tub and a few pans. The plantation owners lived in great style and luxury. Most of them owned a good many slaves. The Negroes were little removed from savagery when they were first brought here, but they made great improvements. After the War freed them from slavery, most of them were a good faithful people. Some have stayed loyal to the families that owned them. Professional people, doctors and dentists and lawyers, lived in Oxford along with the merchants and the tradesmen.

The hill people tried to prosper, and some of them did pretty well making moonshine liquor from corn grown on the poor hills. In some of the creek bottoms they built water mills. The Scotch did most of that. I had an old Scotch uncle, one of the McEachins, who built a mill. He dug the millraces himself and made the water mills and the gears and wheels out·of wood. Some of the old water mills east of Abbeville stood until a few years ago.

In this county there is a kind of salty, down-to-earth folk humor based on tall tales and understatement and old frontier Southern character. Because Lafayette County has remained so rural as it has, the elemental frontier American character has been preserved more than in most other sections of the country and of the South, and even more than in some urban counties in Mississippi. There are more small farmers in this county than there are in the rich section of big farms in the Delta. Faulkner has observed carefully the farmers, the deer hunters, and the Negroes, and in them he has seen a character and quality which has added something to his work peculiarly identifiable with his environment. He would have found something to write about anywhere, but as a citizen of Lafayette County he has known things that he could not have found in many places in the South and that he could hardly have found at all outside the South.

The Civil War had a special effect on the county and Faulkner's works. The South is the only region of the country which has ever been defeated in a war, and this county suffered enough in the War so that it remained especially aware of its tribulations. The county's traditions and its awareness of the past have been the source of some of the conflicts and problems in the fiction. Faulkner and many citizens know the same stories, but interesting as the facts are, Faulkner's stories are infinitely deeper than what most people see when they observe the sources.

In many places, over and over, such as the beginnings of "That Evening Sun" and "A Rose for Emily," Faulkner has pointed out that even in Oxford the small, stereotyped modern home, the service station, and the bloated grape-like things on the power line have replaced more colorful and varied things from the past. Rural life is passing away and industrial, mechanized, civilized life is coming even into Lafayette County. Faulkner seems to think this is a great loss, not in every way, of course, but in many ways. We will miss the old things. There will come a time when Oxford will have lost the character that it has in Faulkner's writings. People will not be as interested in each other as they have been in the past, and that will be a great loss. Neighborliness is already fading out. Sitting up with sick people and with the dying and the dead is a lost custom. Today the sick go to the hospital, and sometimes they have a few visitors. People do not have time any more. Faulkner wrote about the years when people did have time for each other and when they knew how to enjoy life even though they had a harder life. Faulkner's world was not cluttered up with so many people as it is today. The way the men raised hell and had a good time at a horse auction could not happen any more. Now instead of going to a horse auction, a man would go to a used-car lot. There is not now the sense of humor and fun that the old people had in horse-trading. A man gets cheated at the used-car lot in the same way that Flem Snopes cheated the people, but there is no fun to go with it. If Faulkner were born in Lafayette County today, it would not be nearly so auspicious a time as actually when he was born near the beginning of the century. Even hunting in the Delta has changed. If Ike McCaslin went into the Big Bottom in 1959 when he was eleven years old, instead of in the 1870's, he would find fields rather than the great virgin timber. Instead of the old-time woodsmen and sportsmen, there are dude hunters. The old world that Faulkner described is like an old, solitary deer stand. The modern world is like a deer stand on a highway.

Time and place have been important in Faulkner's works. If they were removed, we cannot imagine what his fiction would be. Much of the excellence of his works is derived from Oxford and Lafayette County and their traditions and their past.